Leslie Linsley's Country Christmas Crafts

Books by Leslie Linsley

Nantucket Style

Key West Houses

Hooked Rugs

Weekend Decorating

The Weekend Quilt

More Weekend Quilts

A Quilter's Country Christmas

Country Weekend Patchwork Quilts

First Steps in Quilting

First Steps in Stenciling

First Steps in Counted Cross-Stitch

America's Favorite Quilts

Country Decorating with Fabric Crafts

A Rainbow of Afghans

Carry-Along Crochet

Quick and Easy Knit & Crochet

Afghans to Knit & Crochet

Leslie Linsley's Christmas Ornaments and Stockings

Leslie Linsley's Night Before Christmas Craft Book

Custom Made

Making It Personal with Monograms, Initials and Names

Army/Navy Surplus: A Decorating Source

The Great Bazaar

Million Dollar Projects from the 5 & 10¢ Store

Photocrafts

New Ideas for Old Furniture

Fabulous Furniture Decorations

Decoupage: A New Look at an Old Craft

The Decoupage Workshop

Decoupage on . . . Wood, Metal, Glass

Wildcrafts

Decoupage for Young Crafters

Air Crafts: Playthings to Make & Fly

Scrimshaw: A Traditional Folk Art, a Contemporary Craft

Leslie Linsley's
Country Christmas Crafts

More than 50 Quick-and-Easy Projects
to Make for Holiday Gifts, Decorations, Stockings,
and Tree Ornaments

Leslie Linsley

Photographs by Jon Aron

St. Martin's Griffin

New York

Book design and photography: Jon Aron

Artwork: Peter Peluso
Robby Savonen
Jeffrey Terr

LESLIE LINSLEY'S COUNTRY CHRISTMAS CRAFTS. Copyright © 1995, 1993, 1990, 1987, 1986, 1985, 1984, 1983 by Leslie Linsley. All rights reserved. Printed in the United Stated of America. No part of this book may be used or reproduced in any manner whatsoever without written permission except in the case of brief quotations embodied in critical articles or reviews. For information, address St. Martin's Press, 175 Fifth Avenue, New York, N.Y. 10010.

ISBN 0-312-13535-1

First St. Martin's Griffin Edition: November 1995

10 9 8 7 6 5 4 3 2 1

Contents

Gifts for Children 93

Christmas Stockings 113

Christmas Ornaments 131

Leslie Linsley's Country Christmas Crafts

Introduction

It's no secret that most of us love to make things for the holidays. It's an excuse to decorate our homes, make tree ornaments and stockings, and give gifts that are an expression of ourselves. The fact that the Christmas season begins the day after Thanksgiving and doesn't end until New Year's Day makes it all the more fun. We get to enjoy the decorations for an entire month.

I've written over forty-five books on all different crafts, but none has been as satisfying as those about crafting for Christmas. A few years ago my daughter and I worked on a book together, *Christmas Treasures*, by Robby Smith. We never had so much fun as when we were designing and making the projects for that book.

This year all three of my daughters decorated their trees with ornaments we made together over the years. Now that they have their own homes they've begun to add their own ornaments and decorations. It's especially gratifying to see how they are carrying on the tradition of holiday crafting. We love remembering Christmases past as we hang each ornament or decorate the mantelpiece with the storybook characters we made when they were little.

Every project in this book is represented many times over, in many different versions, in all of our homes. The Noel Banner hangs on the wall in Lisa's entry hall. We had our Christmas breakfast on Amy's Holiday Place Mats, and Robby's tree is covered with Cookie Cutter Ornaments. Everyone's tree is festooned with an assortment of Angel Cats and my all-time favorite, Ribbon Stars.

Friends and acquaintances often ask how I keep coming up with new ideas. My antennae are always up. While I'm making one thing I'm usually thinking about other projects that might work with the same technique. As a craft designer, I'm drawn to expensive boutiques for stimulation. Sometimes I come across something that doesn't relate to Christmas at all. It might be a sachet made from scraps of pastel fabric, lace, and buttons. Somewhere a bell goes off and in my mind I begin to redesign that item in red and green fabrics, adding some of my own touches to turn it into an ornament or holiday gift.

I think about Christmas all year long and often start making things as early as July. In this way I extend the fun of crafting, making it a leisurely, rather than a frantic activity. This gives me time to plan ahead. I'll work on a quilt, for example, and then set aside the fabric scraps for making ornaments closer to the holidays.

Anyone who has ever made anything knows that the joy of making something to give as a gift goes beyond the creative experience. Watching someone open something you've made is a real pleasure. Everyone appreciates the thoughtfulness that's delivered with a handmade gift. You know the recipient will keep and treasure it and enjoy it over and over again.

So, even if you feel all thumbs at any other time of the year, Christmas brings out the urge in all of us to make something festive. This is the time to take out all your odds and ends: ribbons, sequins, fabric scraps, buttons, paint, stencils, and other craft materials. Put on some Christmas music, make cider, eggnog, or a good cup of tea, and settle in for a day of crafting. You will feel incredibly satisfied from your endeavors.

The following terms will help you understand how a project is made. This information will also help you with the sewing construction of each project. These are basic and logical terms and explanations, and if you are new to the world of crafting, they will enable you to see how easy it is.

Appliqué: the technique of creating a design by cutting a shape from one fabric and stitching it to a contrasting fabric background. See Crafting Techniques for more detail.

Backing: the piece of fabric used on the underside of the pieced or appliquéd top of a project. Usually of the same weight fabric, this piece can be made from solid or printed fabric to match the top design. Sometimes the backing is made from the same fabric as that used to create the borders on a quilt or wall-hanging. I especially like to use an old sheet for the backing on a quilt. The sizes are large enough without adding seams for piecing an old sheet is nice and soft. When making small projects, one of the fabric pieces from the top can be used for the backing. In this way the project is completely coordinated.

Basting: securing the top, batting, and backing together with long, loose stitches before quilting. These stitches are removed after each section is quilted. See Crafting Techniques for more detail.

Batting: the soft lining that make a quilted project puffy and gives a quilt warmth. Batting comes in various thicknesses, each appropriate for different kinds of projects. Most quilts are made with a thin layer of Poly-Fil. This thin layer of batting is also used between the top and backing of a pillow that is being quilted. Batting also comes in small, fluffy pieces that are used for projects that require stuffing, such as sachets, ornaments, pin cushions, pillows, etc.

Binding: the way the raw edges of fabric are finished. Contrasting fabric or bias binding is also used. Binding comes prepackaged in various widths and colors and can be used for a quick and easy way to finish the top edge of a Christmas stocking.

Block: this is also referred to as a square. Geometric or symmetrical pieces of fabric are sewn together to create a design. The finished blocks are then joined to create the finished quilt or wallhanging top. Individual blocks are often large enough to use for a pillow. A series of small blocks can be joined to create an interesting pattern for a wallhanging or bench cushion, and for many other projects.

Borders: fabric strips that frame the pieced design. A border can be narrow or wide depending on the size of the project, and sometimes there is more than one border around a quilt, pillow, or wallhanging. Borders often frame quilt blocks and can be made from one of the fabrics in the block, or from a contrasting fabric. Borders can be used around a center patchwork design for a project as small as a pot holder. When making small projects like wall banners, a quilting pattern in the border adds interest to the patchwork top.

Patchwork: sewing together fabric pieces to create an entire design. Sometimes the shapes form a geometric block. The blocks are then sewn together to make up the completed project.

Piecing: joining patchwork pieces together to form a design on the block.

Quilting: stitching together two layers of fabric with a layer of batting between. See Crafting Techniques for more detail on different types of quilting.

Quilting Patterns: the lines or markings on the fabric that make up the design. Small hand or machine stitches quilt along these lines, which might be straight or curved or made up of elaborate curlicued patterns. Small quilting stitches can also follow the seam lines where pieces of fabric are joined. Or a quilting pattern can be created by stitching a grid or diamonds over the entire fabric.

Sash or Strips: the narrow pieces of fabric used to frame individual blocks and join them together. They are often created in a contrasting color.

Setting: joining quilt blocks to form the finished top of a quilt.

Template: a pattern that is rigid and full size. It can be cut from cardboard or plastic and is used to trace the design elements. Some crafters use sandpaper for their templates because they are of the acceptable weight and won't slide on the fabric. When cutting the fabric, you will usually add ¼ inch for seam allowance. When the pattern piece for any project in this book calls for a template, it will state if seam allowance is included.

Supplies

Fabric: You can never have too many different fabric patterns when designing a sewing project. Fabric is the main concern: what kind, how much to buy, and what colors or prints will work together.

Almost every type of fabric has been used for making craft projects. Most crafters prefer cotton, however, and, if necessary, will settle for a cotton/polyester blend in order to find the right color or pattern for the project. Pure cotton should be washed before it is used. This removes any sizing in the fabric and allows for shrinkage.

When collecting a variety of fabric prints for your projects, it's a good idea to have a selection of lights and darks. The contrasts of fabric color and pattern will greatly affect the design. Calico has always been popular. These small, overall prints can be used effectively together and there is a wide variety of colors to choose from.

Iron: An iron is indispensable for any sewing project. Every stitching step is followed by the directions to press seams. If you are doing patchwork, for example, it's handy to pad a stool or chair with a piece of batting and place it next to you by the sewing machine. As you piece the fabric you can iron the seams without getting up.

Needles: All the sewing projects in this book can be stitched on a sewing machine. If stitching by hand, you will need #7 and #8 sharps, which are the most common sizes. They are often called "between."

Ruler and Yardstick: These are a must. A metal ruler can be used as a straightedge for the most accurate cutting. Use the yardstick for cutting lengths of fabric where you must mark the cut at least 36 inches at one time.

The width of the yardstick is often used to mark a grid pattern for quilting. You simply draw the first line, then flip the yardstick over and continue to mark lines without ever removing the yardstick from the fabric. You will have a perfect 1-inch grid.

Scissors: Good-quality scissors are essential for accurately cutting your fabric. Do not use your fabric scissors for cutting paper. This will ruin your scissors.

Templates: Shirt board or the manila oak tag used for filing folders is ideal for use to cut templates. Acetate is also a good material because you'll get clean, crisp edges and you can see through it. These sturdy templates are used for appliqué pieces when a repeat design is required, such as for making the Noel Banner (page 24) or the No-Sew Apple Collage (page 48). If you are cutting only one design, you can simply use the paper pattern pinned to the fabric as a cutting guide.

Thimble: If a project requires quilting, you will be taking 3 to 6 stitches at a time through layers of fabric. It takes a while to get used to using a thimble, but most quilters find it makes this task more fun and painless.

Thread: Match the thread to the color of the fabric. Cotton-blend thread is best for appliqué and piecing.

Basic stitches

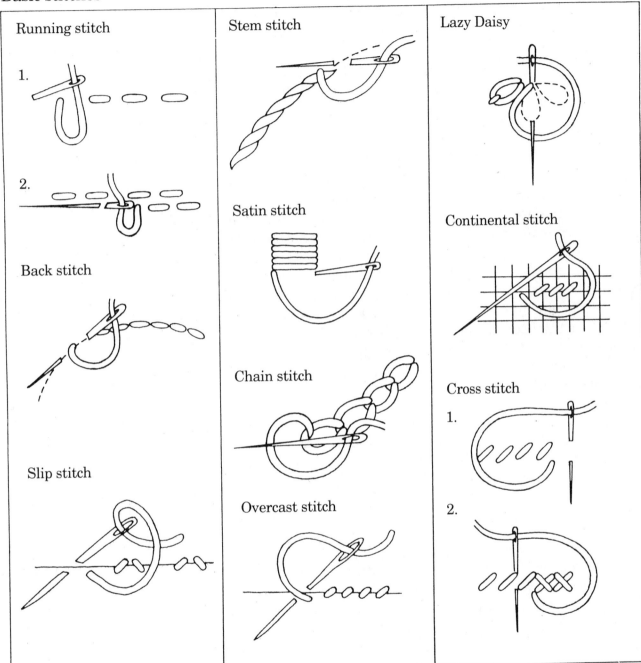

Running stitch

1.

2.

Back stitch

Slip stitch

Stem stitch

Satin stitch

Chain stitch

Overcast stitch

Lazy Daisy

Continental stitch

Cross stitch

1.

2.

Estimating Amount of Fabric

The fabric used for all the projects here is 45 inches wide. All measurements are figured with a $\frac{1}{4}$-inch seam allowance. The amount of materials needed for all projects in the book has been figured out and listed at the beginning of each project, but it's always a good idea to buy a little extra to allow for any cutting or stitching errors.

Enlarging a Design

Whenever possible I try to present patterns full size. However, sometimes it will be necessary to enlarge a pattern that simply wouldn't fit on a page of the book. If you want to enlarge or decrease the size of a pattern piece or design, you can do so on a photocopying machine. If a pattern (such as one for a Christmas stocking) is too large for the page, it will be shown on a grid. Each square on the grid equals 1 inch. This means that you will transfer or copy the design onto graph paper marked with 1-inch squares. Begin by counting the number of squares on the pattern in the book. Number them horizontally and again, vertically. Count the same number of squares on your larger graph and number them in the same way. Copy the design onto your grid one square at a time.

Transferring a Design

Trace the pattern pieces from the book. Place a piece of dressmaker's tracing (carbon) paper on the right side of the fabric with the carbon side down and tracing paper on top. Go over all pattern lines with a tracing wheel or ballpoint pen to transfer the design. Remove the carbon and tracing.

Making a Template

With a pencil, trace the design or pattern on plain paper. Mark each piece with an identifying mark or number and note the number of fabric pieces to be cut from this pattern piece. You can use the pattern piece by pinning it to the corresponding fabric and cutting it out or you can mount it to cardboard with spray adhesive. Apply the glue to the back of the pattern piece, place it firmly on a piece of cardboard or oak tag slightly larger than the pattern piece, and smooth down with your hand. Cut around the pattern to make your template. You can also make a template from clear acetate. Place a piece of acetate over the pattern and trace around the design with a pen as you would on tracing paper. Cut out the exact shape, which includes a ¼-inch seam allowance for all patterns in this book.

Determine which fabric will be used for each template. Consider the grain of the fabric and the direction of the print when placing your templates. Lay the template on the fabric, hold firmly in position, and draw around the outline with a pencil or fabric marker. Mark the back of each piece with the correct number as indicated in the piecing directions. It's a good idea to save templates in an envelope marked with the name of the project.

Sewing Points

Many traditional quilt patterns are created from triangles, diamonds, and similar shapes. The points present a challenge and require special care.

When stitching two such pieces together, sew along the stitch line, but do not sew into the seam allowance at each point. It helps to mark the finished points with a pin so that you can begin and end your seams at these marks.

Sewing Curves

Before turning a curved appliqué piece, stay-stitch along the seam line, then clip or notch evenly spaced cuts along the edge in the seam allowance. Clip all inward curves and notch all outward curves. When the fabric is turned under it will lie flat.

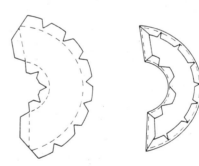

Sewing an Inside Corner Edge

Place a pin across the point of the stitches and clip up to the stitches in the seam allowance in order to turn the fabric under.

Sewing an Outside Corner Edge

Once you've stitched around a corner, clip off half the seam allowance across the point. Turn fabric back, press seams open, and trim excess fabric.

Turning Corners

It's often a bit difficult to turn corners and continue a seam line. Figure 1 shows the three pieces to be joined. With right sides facing, stitch piece A to piece B as shown in Figure 2. Next, join C to A as shown in Figure 3. Leave the needle down in the fabric. Lift the presser foot and clip the seam to the needle. Slide B under C and adjust so the edges of B align with C. Lower the presser foot and stitch along the seam line (Figure 4).

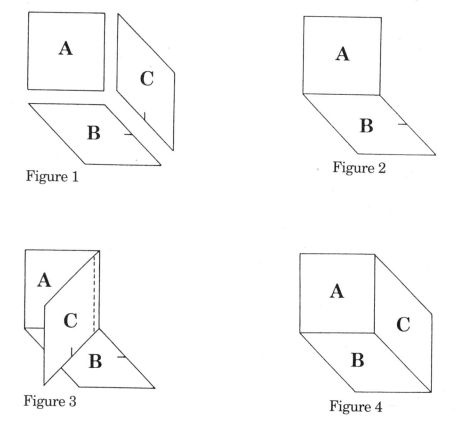

Figure 1

Figure 2

Figure 3

Figure 4

Appliquéing

Using a template, cut out each pattern piece. If there is no seam allowance on your template, add ¼ to ⅜ inch all around when cutting. Place the template on the back of the fabric and press all edges over the template edges. If the appliqué is curved, clip all edges to seam line before turning.

Pin the appliqué in place on the background fabric and blind-stitch or whip-stitch it all around. The appliquéd fabric is then backed with batting before you quilt around the design.

Use short running stitches around the inside edge of the appliqué.

To machine-stitch appliqué, cut the fabric without seam allowance. Edges need not be turned. Pin the appliqué in position on the fabric and zigzag-stitch around the edges.

Hem Stitch

This is often used to finish the edges of appliqué. Use thread to match the fabric. Bring the needle up from the wrong side of the fabric through the folded edge of the appliqué. Insert the needle on the diagonal into the top of the fabric close to the appliqué and slightly ahead of the first stitch.

Quilting

Quilting is the means by which you sew layers of fabric and batting together to produce a padded fabric held together by stitching. The quilting process, generally the finishing step in appliqué and patchwork projects, is what makes a project interesting and gives it a textured look.

Basting

Before quilting you will baste the quilt or wallhanging top, batting, and backing together. To avoid a lump of filler at any point, begin at the center of the top and baste outward with long, loose stitches, thus creating a sunburst pattern. There should be about 6 inches between the basted lines at the edges of the quilt. Baste from the top only. These stitches will be cut away as you do your quilting.

Hand Quilting

Thread your needle and knot one end as for regular hand sewing. Bring the needle up through the back to the front and give the knotted end a good tug to pull it through the backing fabric into the batting. Keep your thread fairly short (about 18 inches) and take small running stitches. Follow your premarked quilting pattern.

Machine Quilting

This is a quicker way to create a quilted look, but machine-quilted projects do not have the same, rich look of authentic, early quilting that hand-stitched projects have. It is best to machine-quilt when the batting isn't too thick. When small pieces of fabric are stitched together to make a patchwork project, machine quilting is quick and easy.

Outline Quilting

This is the method of quilting just outside the line of your appliquéd designs or along the patchwork seams. In this way, each design element is pronounced and the layers of fabric are secure.

Overall Quilting

When you want to cover the fabric with quilting, choose a simple design. The background quilting should not interfere with the patchwork or appliqué elements.

To ensure accurate spacing, make grid patterns of squares or diamond shapes with a yardstick or masking tape. For a quick and easy method, lay a yardstick diagonally across the fabric and mark the material with a light pencil. Without removing the yardstick, turn it over and mark along the edge once again. Continue across the fabric to the opposite edge. You will have perfect 1-inch spaces between each line. Lay the yardstick across the fabric at the corner opposite to where you began and repeat the process to create a 1-inch grid across the top of the fabric as we did with the Around-the-World Quilt (page 38). Stitch along these lines with small running stitches. The stitching will hide the pencil lines.

Counted Cross-Stitch

Each square on the design represents an X stitch on fabric. You simply count the number of squares on your chart and work them in a corresponding manner on an even-weave fabric such as Hardanger or Aida (available in needlework and craft shops). Use a blunt-end embroidery needle, an embroidery hoop to keep the work taut, and 6-strand embroidery floss. Stitch all lines slanted in the same direction and then the other. All top threads should cross over in the same direction. Some projects will require all 6 strands; others look best with 2 or 3. Begin each project by separating the strands and putting together the numbers required. Use lengths of thread that feel comfortable to work with.

Pillow Piping

Contrasting or matching piping is a nice way to finish the edges of a pillow or ornament. Projects have a crisp and professional look when trimmed with matching fabric-covered piping. Piping can be very narrow for a small ornament, or quite fat, if used on an oversized throw pillow. The cording for piping is sold by the yard in most fabric shops and is fairly inexpensive. It looks like soft rope.

To pipe, measure around the project and add an extra inch. Cut lengths of fabric, on the bias, 1½ inches wide and stitch them together to create a strip long enough to go around the project with an extra inch.

Place the cording in the center of the strip. Fold the fabric over the cording so the long, raw edges meet, with the cord encased inside.

Using a zipper foot on your sewing machine, stitch along the fabric as close to the cording as possible. When you get to the end, turn the raw fabric edge under, but do not stitch the last half hind of the fabric together.

Begin at the center of one edge of the top fabric and pin the piping all around. Where the two ends meet, overlap the extra fabric so the cording comes together inside the fabric channel. Stitch around.

Slip Stitching

When closing seams, the slip stitch is usually recommended because it is invisible. Fold under the seam allowance on one side of the opening and pin it over the raw edges of the opposite side of the fabric.

Insert the needle through the bottom layer of the fabric right at the seam line at one end of the opening. Take a small stitch through the fold on the top layer, then through the seam line on the bottom layer. Continue in this way so that the seam line matches the area that has been machine stitched from the wrong side.

Quick-and-Easy Triangle Method

This is a quick and easy way to join light and dark triangles to create squares of any size. Once you've determined the size of your finished unit, add 1 inch to it. For example, if you want to create 2-inch squares, use a yardstick to mark off 3-inch squares on the wrong side of your light fabric.

Next, draw diagonal lines through all squares as shown in the top diagram. With right sides facing and raw edges aligned, pin the marked light fabric to the same-size dark fabric. Stitch a ¼-inch seam on each side of the drawn diagonal lines as shown.

Cut on all solid lines to get the individual units of light and dark fabric triangles. Clip the corners, open, and press.

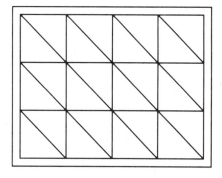

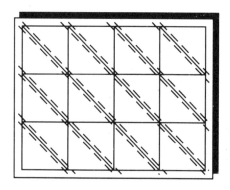

Christmas Wallhangings, Banners, and Wreaths

Noel Banner

Decorate your front door or entrance hallway for the holidays with this colorful Christmas banner. It's easy to make the appliqués with fusible webbing, calico, and iron-on felt. No stitching required! The finished banner is 22 x 24 inches.

Materials
¼ yard green calico
⅔ yard white Christmas calico
1 yard red calico for backing
small amount of blue calico
small piece each of red and green iron-on felt, or regular felt used
   with fusible webbing
fusible webbing
1 yard thin quilt batting
tracing paper
stiff paper for template
ballpoint pen
Velcro tabs for hanging

Directions
The pattern pieces for this project are given full size; therefore, no enlarging is necessary. Because the appliqués are fused to the fabric background, there is no seam allowance.

1. Begin by tracing and transferring the pattern pieces to stiff paper (page 16).
2. Place each letter template on red felt and draw around the outline with a ballpoint pen.
3. Trace around the circle template to make 3 berries.
4. Using holly pattern piece A on green calico, draw around outline to make 3.
5. Using holly pattern piece B on green felt, draw around outline to make 3.
6. Place the bow pattern on the fold of the blue calico fabric where indicated on the pattern. Pin and trace around template.
7. Pin all fabric pieces, except iron-on felt, if used, to fusible webbing.

To cut

1. Cut out all appliqué pieces, keeping them pinned to the fusible webbing.
2. Cut white Christmas calico 19½ x 21½ inches.
3. Cut 2 strips of green calico 2 x 21½ inches. Cut 2 strips of green

Figure 1

calico 2 x 19½ inches.

4. Cut 4 red calico squares 2 x 2 inches.

5. Cut quilt batting 21½ x 23½ inches.

6. Cut backing fabric 22½ x 24¼ inches.

To assemble

1. Arrange all appliqué pieces in position on the white fabric as shown in Figure 1.

2. Fuse each piece in position, using a medium-hot iron and following directions on the package.

3. With right sides facing and raw edges aligned, join a long green calico strip to the top and bottom edges of the white calico piece. Open seams and press.

4. With right sides facing and raw edges aligned, join a red calico square to each short end of the remaining calico strips. Open seams and press.

5. With right sides facing and raw edges aligned, join these strips to each side of the white fabric top. Open seams and press.

To finish

1. With wrong sides facing, pin the top fabric to the backing with the batting between.

2. Machine-stitch along seam lines of the border through all 3 layers.

3. Turn all raw edges under to inside ¼ inch and press. Slip-stitch all around to finish edges.

4. Hang with Velcro tabs.

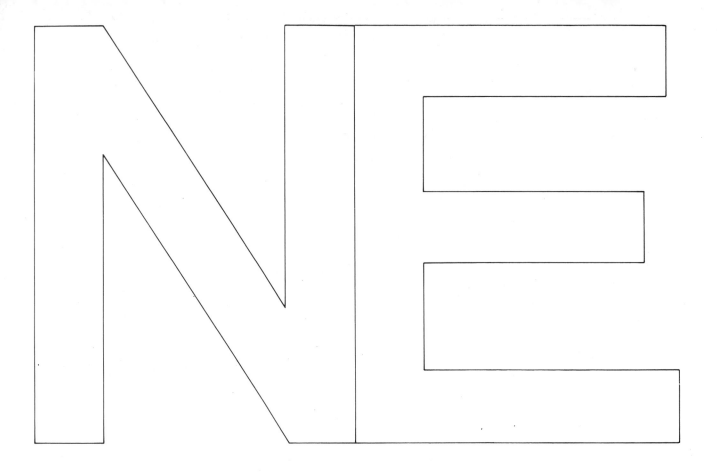

Noel Banner letters

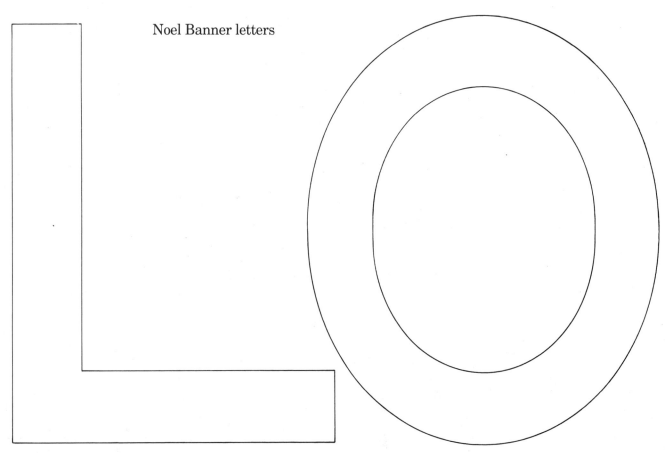

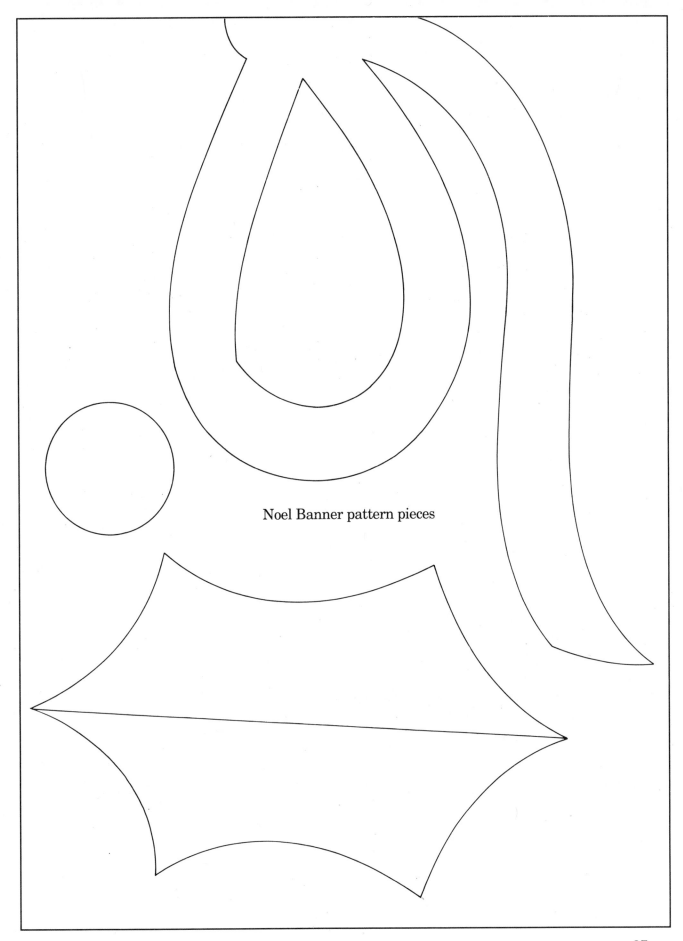

Noel Banner pattern pieces

Country Heart Wreath

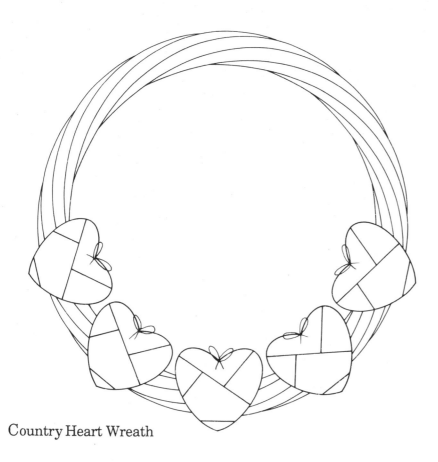

Country Heart Wreath

Wreaths made of honeysuckle, grapevines, and other natural materials provide a country welcome at Christmastime. Some people hang them all year long. They are easy to find at most garden shops and come in several sizes.

The patchwork hearts add a personal touch and are lots of fun to make. Make 5 for the wreath and more for delightful Christmas tree ornaments. They are also good sachets when filled with potpourri. This is the perfect small gift to bring when visiting during the holidays.

Materials
grapevine wreath
small amount of green fabric
small amounts of 4 different red calicos
small amount of white Christmas calico
Poly-Fil stuffing
tracing paper
stiff paper

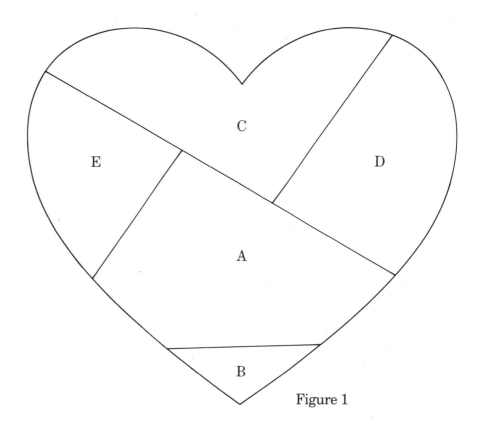

Figure 1

Directions

All patterns include a ¼-inch seam allowance.

1. Trace heart pattern and pieces and transfer to stiff paper for templates (page 16).

2. Cut 5 different red calico hearts for backings.

3. Cut 5 A pieces out of the green fabric.

4. Cut 5 B, C, D, and E pieces out of different red and white calicos, so you have a variety of pieces.

5. Arrange pattern pieces to make up 5 hearts (Figure 1).

6. With right side facing and raw edges aligned, stitch all A pieces to all B pieces. Open seams and press.

7. With right sides facing and raw edges aligned, stitch all C pieces to D pieces. Join all E pieces to A as shown in Figure 1. Open seams and press.

8. Join sections C-D to sections B-A-E. Open seams and press. You will have 5 crazy-quilt patchwork hearts. If desired, you can add decorative cross stitches along all joining seams of patchwork to give each heart a country look (page 20).

9. With right sides facing and raw edges aligned, pin each patchwork heart to backing. Stitch around all hearts, leaving a small opening for turning and stuffing.

10. Trim around seams and turn hearts right-side out.

11. Stuff hearts tightly, turn raw edges under, and slip-stitch opening closed.

12. Arrange stuffed hearts on wreath and tack in position. Decorate wreath with red ribbons, small ornaments, and pinecones, if desired.

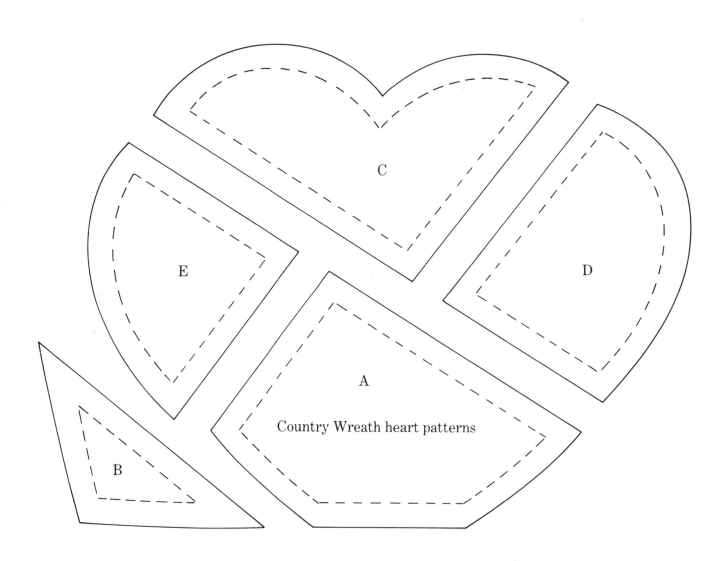

Country Wreath heart patterns

Braided Wreath

It takes 3 long strips of red, green, and white Christmas fabric to make this braided wreath. Add a big red bow, some pinecones, bells, ribbons, or tiny balls for a festive door decoration.

A creative use for this project is as a punch bowl holder. Make the wreath to fit the diameter of your punch bowl. Place the wreath on a table with the bow in front and set the punch bowl in the center.

Materials
¼ yard red calico
¼ yard solid green
¼ yard white Christmas calico
Poly-Fil stuffing
4-inch-wide red ribbon for bow
decorations such as pinecones, tiny balls, ribbons, bells, etc.

Directions
All measurements for cutting fabric include a ¼-inch seam allowance.

Cut the following:
red calico

       1 strip 6 x 45 inches

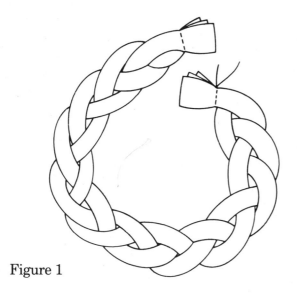

Figure 1

green calico
      1 strip 6 x 45 inches
white calico
      1 strip 6 x 45 inches

To assemble

1. With right sides facing and raw edges aligned, fold each strip in half lengthwise and press.
2. Stitch along the long edge and across one end.
3. Trim seam and turn right-side out.
4. Stuff each tube firmly with stuffing.
5. Pin the open ends of all 3 tubes together.
6. Braid the tubes together and form the braid into a circle. Stitch the ends together (Figure 1).
7. Turn the wreath so that the stitched ends are at the top.
8. Make a fat bow with the wide ribbon and secure it over the joined ends. Add decorations all around if desired.
9. If you are making this project as a punch bowl holder, the joined ends with the ribbon bow should be in front and the ends of the ribbon spread on the table or hanging over the front of the buffet.

Calico Teacup Wallhanging

This delightful design is perfect for using up your small scraps of fabric. It's fun to design this project because almost any color combination will look good. Small prints work best on these small appliqué pieces, as do solids.

I like this wallhanging for a kitchen area. The finished size is 34 x 34 inches, but if you want to make it larger or smaller, simply add or subtract blocks. For a holiday theme, choose red, green, and white prints.

Figure 1. Calico Teacup Wallhanging

Materials

scraps of 9 different calico prints
½ yard green calico
¼ yard red fabric
¼ yard plaid fabric
½ yard muslin
1 yard backing fabric
1 yard thin quilt batting
tracing paper
stiff paper for templates

Directions

All measurements include ¼-inch seam allowance.

1. Trace each pattern piece from Figure 3 and transfer to heavy paper (page 16).
2. Pin template pieces for each teacup to 9 different calicos.
3. Cut each calico piece out with an extra ¼ inch all around.

Cut the following:

green: 24 strips 3 x 8½ inches
red: 32 squares 1¾ x 1¾ inches
plaid: 32 squares 1¼ x 1¼ inches
muslin: 9 squares 8½ x 8½ inches
backing: 1 piece 35 x 35 inches

Preparing the appliqués

1. Stay-stitch around the curved edge of each side of the teacup

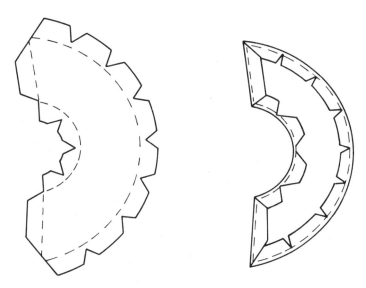

Figure 2. Preparing a curved piece for appliqué

handle (pattern piece 2 in Figure 3), ¼ inch from the edge. Clip around inside curve to stitch line. Notch outside curve to stitch line (Figure 2).

2. Turn both edges under to wrong side along stitch lines and press.

3. With right sides facing and notches matching, pin the handle (pattern piece 2) in place on the cup piece (pattern piece 1). Stitch across each end of the handle. Press seams toward teacup.

4. Place teacup template on wrong side of the fabric; turn and press the raw edges over the edges of the template. Remove cardboard and repress fabric.

5. With right sides facing, center pattern piece 3 on pattern piece 1 and stitch across between edges of the cup. Press seams down toward base of cup.

6. Turn all raw edges of the saucer (pattern piece 3) under ¼ inch and press.

7. Make 9 teacup appliqués in this way.

8. Center and pin an appliqué to each muslin square. Slip-stitch around.

To make rows

1. With right sides facing and raw edges aligned, join a green calico strip to an appliqué square along one side edge. Open seams and press.

2. Continue with another green strip on the opposite side, followed by another appliqué square, then a green strip until you have a row of 3 blocks separated by 4 green lattice strips. Open seams and press.

4. Make 3 rows in this way.

To join rows

1. With right sides facing and raw edges aligned, stitch a red 1¾-inch square to the same size plaid square along one side edge.

2. Reverse the order and join a plaid square to a red square. Join all 4 squares to make a 3-inch red and plaid checkerboard square. Make 16 squares.

3. With right sides facing and raw edges aligned, stitch a square to the short end of a green calico strip, followed by another square, then a calico strip, another square, a calico strip, and a fourth square to make one long strip. Open seams and press. Make 4 of these units.

4. With right sides facing and raw edges aligned, stitch one

pieced strip to the top edge of a row of blocks. Open seams and press.

5. Continue to join rows, separated by strips in this way (Figure 1).

To quilt

1. Pin the appliqué top to the quilt batting and then to the backing fabric.

2. Starting at the center and moving outward in a sunburst pattern, take long, loose stitches to baste the 3 layers of fabric together.

3. Using small running stitches, quilt ¼ inch on each side of all seam lines. Do not stitch into seam allowance of the outside edges.

4. To add more quilting in the borders of each block and around each teacup appliqué, see page 20.

To finish

1. Remove the basting stitches.

2. Trim the batting ¼ inch smaller than the quilt top all around.

3. Trim the backing fabric to the same size as the top.

4. Turn all raw edges to inside ¼ inch all around and pin. Press.

5. Machine-stitch all around, close to outside edges.

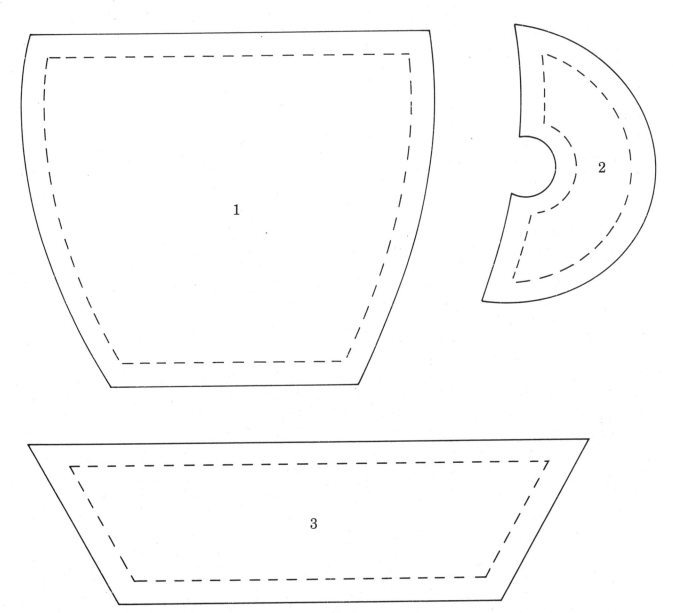

Figure 3. Teacup appliqué pattern pieces

Around-the-World Quilt

Designed by Robby Smith, this is a popular quilt pattern (see photograph in color section). However, the use of primary colors is what gives it vitality. This is a good example of how to use solid, bright colors. The finished wallhanging is 40 x 40 inches. This project would make a nice baby quilt. To enlarge the finished size, add an 8- to 10-inch border all around.

Figure 1. Around-the-World Quilt

Materials (*45-inch-wide fabric*)
2 yards blue fabric (A, includes backing)
¾ yard red fabric (B)
¼ yard green fabric (C)
¼ yard yellow fabric (D)
1¼ yards thin quilt batting
Velcro tabs, for hanging

Directions
All measurements include ¼-inch seam allowance.

Cut the following:
Blue (A)
      48 squares 3 x 3 inches
      backing piece 41 x 41 inches
Red (B)
      24 squares 3 x 3 inches
      2 squares 20¼ x 20¼ inches —cut into 2 triangles each
        (4 triangles)
Green (C)
      24 squares 3 x 3 inches
Yellows (D)
      25 squares 3x 3 inches

To make rows
1. With right sides facing and raw edges aligned, stitch the squares together in the following sequence to make 11 rows:
A-A-B-C-D-A-D-C-B-A-A
A-B-C-D-A-A-A-D-C-B-A
B-C-D-A-A-B-A-A-D-C-B
C-D-A-A-B-C-B-A-A-D-C
D-A-A-B-C-D-C-B-A-A-D
A-A-B-C-D-D-D-C-B-A-A
D-A-A-B-C-D-C-B-A-A-D
C-D-A-A-B-C-B-A-A-D-C
B-C-D-A-A-B-A-A-D-C-B
A-B-C-D-A-A-A-D-C-B-A
A-A-B-C-D-A-D-C-B-A-A
2. Open all seams and press.

To join rows

1. Making sure that all seams line up, with right sides facing and raw edges aligned, join the first two rows along the bottom, long edge.
2. Open seams and press.
3. Continue to join rows in the sequence above.

To finish top

1. With right sides facing and raw edges aligned, stitch the long edge of a red triangle to one side edge of the pieced squares. Open seams and press.
2. Continue to join the other 3 triangles in the same way.

To quilt

1. Trace and transfer the quilting pattern (Figure 2) in position so it is centered on each red triangle (see page 16).
2. Place the top fabric on the batting and then on the backing fabric and pin all 3 layers together.
3. Starting in the center and working outward in a sunburst pattern, take long basting stitches through the fabric.
4. Using small running stitches, quilt ¼ inch on each side of all seam lines. Do not quilt into the seam allowance around the outside edges of the quilt.
5. Quilt in the same way along all marked lines of the transferred quilting pattern.

To finish

1. Remove all basting stitches.
2. Trim the batting so it is same size as quilt top.
3. Fold the edges of the backing under the wrong side ¼ inch and press.
4. Fold the remaining edges of the backing fabric over onto the quilt top and pin all around. Press.
5. Slip-stitch all around.

Figure 2. Quilting pattern. Each square equals 1 inch.

Christmas Star Wallhanging

This holiday banner was created by Susan Fernald Joyce for a raffle to benefit A Safe Place, a shelter for women in crisis on Nantucket, where we live. Perhaps this will give you an idea for a similar project to help raise funds for a worthy cause.

The quilted banner measures 38 x 50 inches and can be hung horizontally or vertically. It would look pretty over a fireplace or on a door in an entryway.

Figure 1

Materials
¾ yard white calico (A)
1½ yards red calico (B)
1½ yards green calico (C)
1½ yards backing fabric
thin quilt batting

Directions
All measurements include ¼-inch seam allowance.

Cut the following:
White (A)

> 2 pieces 2½ x 38½ inches (side border strips)
> 4 lattice strips 2½ x 22½ inches
> 3 lattice strips 2½ x 10½ inches
> 24 squares 3 x 3 inches
> 24 squares 2¾ x 2¾ inches —cut into 2 triangles each
> > (48 triangles)

Red (B)

> borders
> > 2 pieces 4½ x 29½ inches (top and bottom)
> > 2 pieces 4½ x 49½ inches (sides)
> 6 squares 5½ x 5½ inches
> 24 squares 2¼ x 2¼ inches

Green (C)

> inner borders
> > 2 pieces 2 x 26½ inches (top and bottom)
> > 2 pieces 2 x 41½ inches (sides)
> outer borders
> > 2 pieces 1 x 37½ inches (top and bottom)
> > 2 pieces 1 x 50½ inches (sides)
> 24 squares 3½ x 3½ inches, each cut into 2 triangles
> > (48 triangles)

To make blocks
With right sides facing and raw edges aligned, stitch a white (A) triangle to 2 opposite sides of a small red (B) square to make a larger triangle (Figure 2). Make 4.

Next, stitch the long edge of a green (C) triangle to each short edge of this piece to make a rectangle (Figure 2). Make 4.

Figure 3. With right sides facing and raw edges aligned, stitch

these pieces to each side of a large red (B) square, with a white
(A) square in each corner as shown in Figure 3. Make 3 blocks
in this way and then 3 blocks by reversing the colors and using
red calico for the green and green for the red.

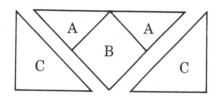

Figure 2

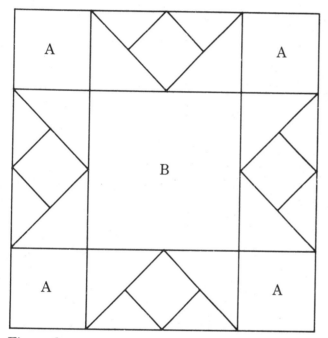

Figure 3

To make a row
1. With right sides facing and raw edges aligned, stitch a block
to white lattice strip (2½ x 10½ inches) along one side. Open
seams and press.
2. With right sides facing and raw edges aligned, join another
block in this way. Open seams and press.
3. Continue to make 3 rows in this way.

To join rows

1. With right sides facing and raw edges aligned, stitch a long white lattice strip (2½ x 22½ inches) to the top edge of a row. Open seams and press.
2. Continue to join rows, separated by a lattice strip, in this way.
3. Attach the bottom lattice strip in the same way (Figure 1).

Borders

1. With right sides facing and raw edges aligned, join the top and bottom, green inner borders. Open seams and press.
2. With right sides facing and raw edges aligned, join the side, inner green borders. Open seams and press.
3. Next, stitch the red top and bottom pieces and then the red side pieces in the same way.
4. Finish by joining the green outer top and bottom borders, then the green side borders (Figure 1).

To quilt

1. Trace and transfer the leaf quilt pattern (Figure 4) to the white lattice strips (page 16).
2. Trace and transfer the bow pattern (Figure 5) to the red borders.
3. Pin the top fabric to the batting and then to the backing.
4. Starting in the center and moving outward in a sunburst pattern, baste all 3 layers together.
5. Using small running stitches, quilt along marked lines. Do not quilt into ¼-inch seam allowance all around.

To finish

1. Remove basting stitches.
2. Trim batting ¼ inch smaller than quilt top.
3. Trim backing to same size as quilt top.
4. Turn raw edges to the inside ¼ inch, press, and machine-stitch or slip-stitch all around.

Figure 4. Quilting pattern for Christmas Wallhanging

Figure 5. Quilting pattern for Christmas Wallhanging

No-Sew Apple Collage

This appliqué picture is created without the usual work involved with appliqués. Each apple is created with scraps of fabric and fusible webbing for a delightful country picture. Hang it in your kitchen or family room to brighten any wall. The finished size is 20 x 22 inches.

Materials
¾ yard muslin
¼ yard 45-inch-wide dark blue print for the border
fusible webbing
pencil, tracing paper, and thin cardboard
scraps of red and green fabric
20 x 22-inch frame and backing

Directions
1. Draw a rectangle 20 x 22 inches on the muslin. Cut 4 strips of dark blue fabric 2½ x 22 inches and 4 matching strips of fusible webbing.

2. Arrange the border strips along the inside of the drawn lines with the webbing between the fabric and the muslin. The corner will overlap.

3. Trace the apple pattern and transfer to thin cardboard such as a manila folder. Cut out and use this as a template to draw 16 apples on the red and green scrap fabric pieces.

4. Pin each fabric piece to fusible webbing and cut out. Cut 16 leaves and stems the same way.

5. Mark off 4 evenly spaced rows across and down on the muslin, using a pencil dot or pin to indicate lines. Arrange the apples so you have 4 rows of 4 on the muslin and fuse with a hot iron. Fuse a leaf and stem with each apple.

6. Cut the muslin about 2 inches outside the blue borders. Spread the picture over the frame backing and pull the extra muslin to the back. Use masking tape to hold in place and frame the picture.

Gifts for the Home

Christmas Lap Quilt

It's always fun to make a quilted wallhanging for the holidays. Star patterns are among the most popular, and you can make this one with the red, white, and green print as shown here for the holidays, or choose colors to match your room and use it all year long. My mother, Ruth Linsley, made this and it was the first time she'd used the quick-and-easy triangle piecing method. Now she says she'll never piece triangles any other way. The finished size is 43 x 43 inches.

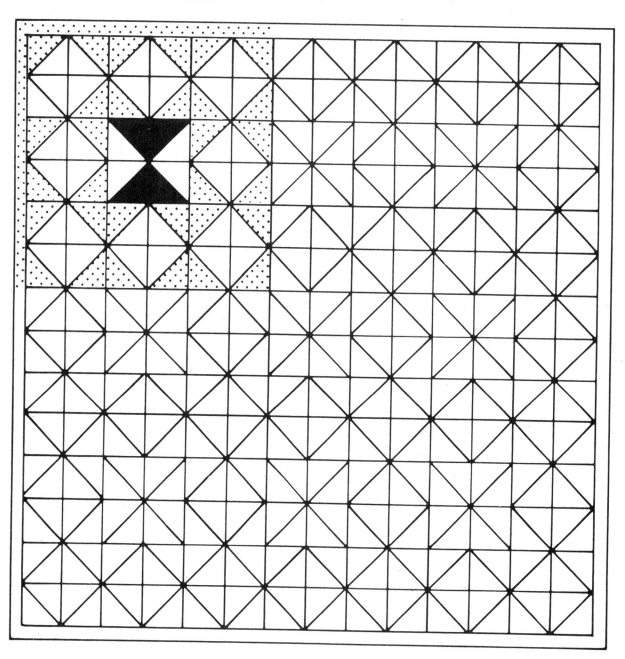

Materials

(all fabric is 45 inches wide)
1 yard green print fabric
1½ yards white fabric
2 yards red print fabric (includes backing)
quilt batting 45 x 45 inches
quilt marker

Directions

All measurements include a ¼-inch seam allowance.

Quick-and-easy triangle method

1. On the wrong side of the white fabric, measure and mark a grid of 80 squares, each 3⅞ x 3⅞ inches, with 8 rows of 10 squares each.

2. With right sides facing, pin this fabric to the same size green fabric. Refer to page 22 for stitching and cutting directions.

3. On the wrong side of the white fabric, measure and mark a grid of 18 squares, each 3⅞ x 3⅞ inches, so you have 6 rows of 3 squares each.

4. With right sides facing, pin this fabric to the same size red fabric. Refer to page 22 for stitching and cutting.

To make a block

Refer to Figure 1 to arrange rows of green/white squares and red/white squares.

1. With right sides facing, join 4 green/white squares to make row 1 as shown. Press seams to one side.

2. Next, join a white/green square to a red/white square along the right-side edge as shown, followed by another red/white square and ending row 2 with a green/white square. Press seams to one side.

3. With right sides facing, join a white/green square to a red/white square, followed by another red/white square and ending row 3 with a green/white square. Press seams to one side.

4. With right sides facing, join 4 green/white squares as shown to make row 4. Press seams to one side.

5. With right sides facing and seams aligned, join the rows to make a block as shown in Figure 2. Make 9 blocks in this way.

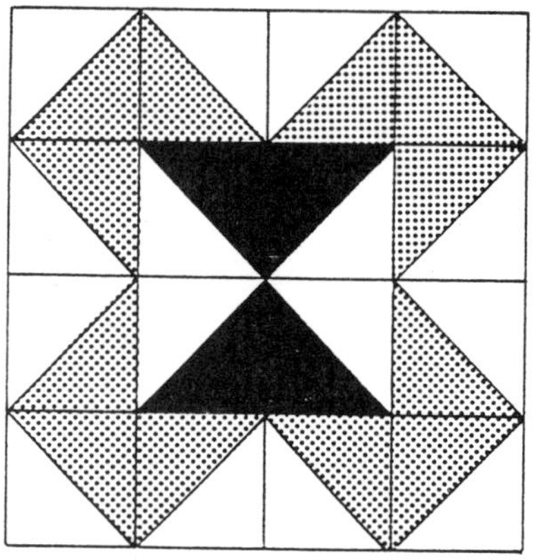

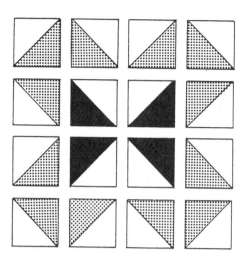

Figure 2

Figure 1

To piece borders
Refer to Figure 3.
1. To make side borders: With right sides facing, join a green/white square to another green/white square along one edge as shown. Press seam to one side.
2. Continue to join 12 squares in this way. Make 2.
3. To make top and bottom borders: With right sides facing, join a green/white square to another green/white square along one edge as shown. Press seam to one side.
4. Continue to join 14 squares in this way. Make 2.

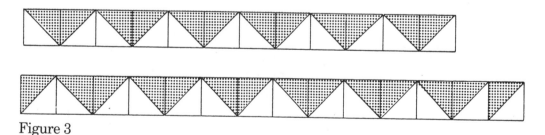

Figure 3

To join blocks
Refer to Figure 4.
1. With right sides facing, join 2 blocks along the right-side edge.

Press seam to one side.

2. Next, join another block in the same way to make a row of 3 blocks.

3. Press seam to one side. Make 3 rows in this way.

To join rows

Refer to Figure 5.

1. With right sides facing and seams aligned, join the bottom edge of the first row to the top edge of the second row.

2. Press seam to one side.

3. Join the last row in the same way.

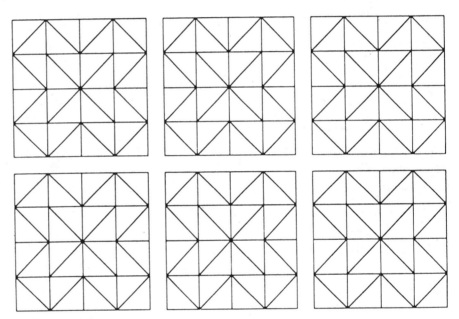

Figure 4

To join borders

Refer to Figure 6.

1. With right sides facing, join a side border strip to the left-side edge of the quilt top as shown.

2. Press seam to one side.

3. Repeat on the opposite side edge.

4. With right sides facing, join a top border strip to the top edge of the quilt as shown.

5. Press seam to one side.

6. Repeat on the bottom edge of the quilt top with the remaining border strip.

To quilt

1. With wrong sides facing and batting between, pin the backing, batting, and quilt top together.

2. Beginning at the center of the quilt and working outward in a sunburst pattern, take long, loose basting stitches through all 3 layers, stopping short of the seam allowance around the outside edges.

3. Take small running stitches ¼ inch from each side of all seam lines, stopping short of the seam allowance around the quilt top.

Figure 5

To finish

1. When all quilting is complete, remove basting stitches.
2. Trim the batting ¼ inch smaller than quilt top all around.
3. Next, turn the raw edges of the backing forward ¼ inch and press.
4. Bring the remaining backing fabric forward to bind the edges of the quilt top and press. Pin all around and slip-stitch to finish the quilt.

Figure 6

Festive Fabric Frame

Use colorful strips of fabric to make a padded mirror frame. This one is 14 x 18 inches, but you can make any size frame and have a mirror cut to size at your local hardware store. The mirror area here is 9 x 13 inches. Or, make this frame to hold a family portrait for a "grandparent" Christmas gift.

Materials
variety of colorful fabric scraps
9 x 13-inch mirror
2 pieces of ⅛-inch Fomecore 14 x 18 inches
14 x 18-inch posterboard
glue
craft knife or razor blade
rubber cement
quilt batting
masking tape
tab for hanging

Directions
1. Cut 40 strips of fabric 1½ x 5½ inches.
2. To make the side borders place one strip face down on top of another and stitch along the 5½-inch edge, leaving a ¼-inch seam allowance. Open and press. Continue to attach strips in this way until you have 12 strips. Repeat.
3. Seam 8 strips together in the same way and make 2 for the top and bottom borders. You will now have 2 patchwork strips 12 inches long and 2 that are 8 inches long.

To assemble
1. Seam a 5½-inch square piece to each end of the 8-inch-long pieces.
2. With right sides facing and raw edges matching, attach a 12-inch-long strip to the top of one square. Open and press. Repeat on the opposite side. Attach the last strip to complete the frame.
3. Center the mirror on the posterboard and draw around the outside edge of the mirror. Cut this with a craft knife and lift out the posterboard center.
4. Glue the posterboard frame, with the mirror set in the center, over one piece of Fomecore. Set aside to dry.
5. From the second piece of Fomecore cut an opening 8½ x 12½ that will frame the mirror.
6. Glue strips of quilt batting to this Fomecore "frame." Place the

fabric frame over the batting and turn the outside raw edges over to the wrong side of the foam frame. Tape the edges down with masking tape. Clip the inside corners to miter them.

7. Next, turn the inside raw edges over to the wrong side of the Fomecore. Tape these edges down so the fabric is taut and smooth on the front. This may require picking up the taped areas and retaping here and there as you work out the wrinkles all around.

To finish

1. Apply rubber cement to the taped back of the fabric frame and to the posterboard around the mounted mirror. Let these pieces dry.

2. Place the fabric frame over the mirror so that the edges of the mirror are covered by the fabric frame all around. Press down. Attach the tab for hanging to the back.

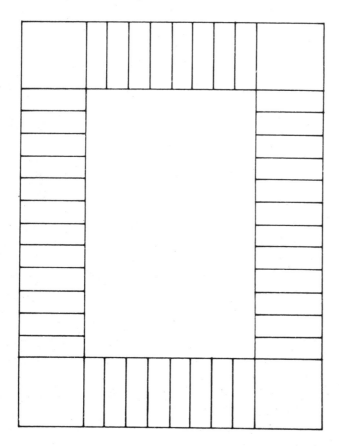

Basket Full of Strawberries

Make a basket filled with large and small strawberry pillows from scraps of different red prints. Place the basket in a hallway for a cheerful greeting or make the little strawberries for Christmas ornaments. They're fun to make in bunches, and when filled with potpourri they make a lasting gift to use year round. Each pillow is 11 inches long and 13½ inches across.

Materials
½ yard fabric for pillow
scraps of red printed fabric for sachets
½ yard green velveteen or corduroy for leaves and stems
brown wrapping paper
piece of white chalk
Poly-Fil stuffing and potpourri mix for sachets
pinking shears
black ballpoint pen
ribbon for hanging

Directions
When selecting fabric, look for calico, gingham, or a tiny print in red or pink colors. Solids are less interesting. The stem and leaves are cut from a plush, textured material, or, if you prefer, these can be cut from a green calico or other small print like gingham.

1. Enlarge pattern (page 16) and transfer to a piece of brown wrapping paper. Pin this to the fabric and draw around it with white chalk. Cut two pieces.

2. With right sides facing, stitch around the strawberry, leaving a 3½-inch opening at the top. Clip around all curved edges to the seam line. Turn right side out and press.

3. Cut 2 pieces for the stem and 10 leaf pieces. With right sides facing, stitch around the edges of the stem, leaving the bottom edge open. Stitch each of the leaves in the same way, leaving a 1½-inch opening at the side of one point. Clip edges. Turn right side out.

To finish
1. Stuff the pillow so it is very full. Stuff the stem and stitch across the bottom. Using a needle and thread, gather the

For pattern on opposite page, each square equals 1 inch

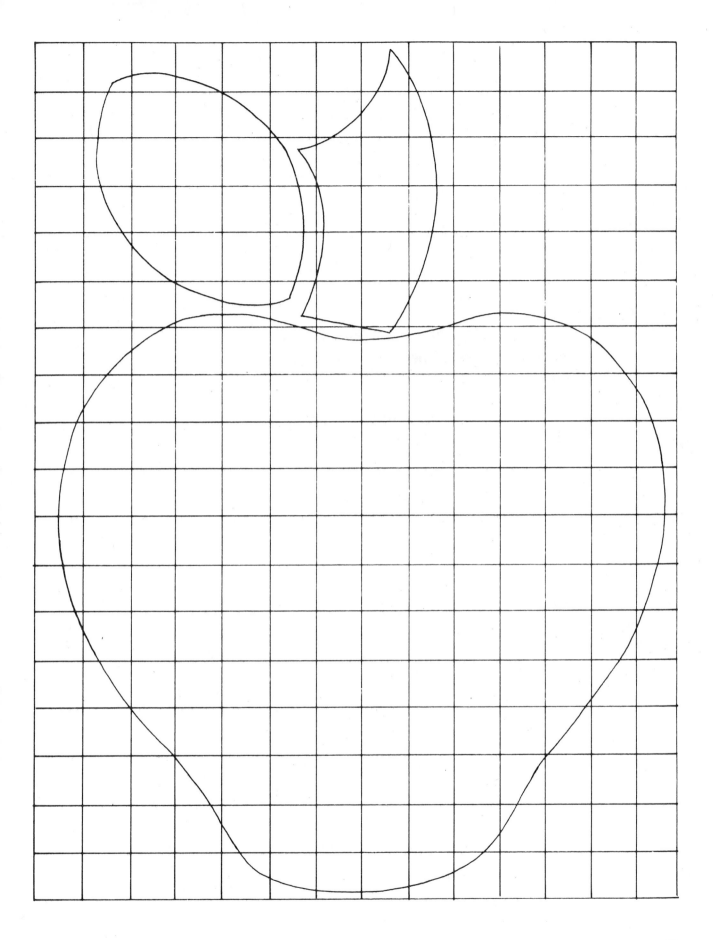

opening around the top of the strawberry opening so there is enough room to stuff the end of the stem into the hole. Insert one end of the stem and stitch together. Each square equals 1 inch.

2. Stuff each of the leaves so they are full but not too plump. Slip-stitch the opening of each leaf closed.

3. Set the sewing machine for a basting stitch and run the machine down the center of each leaf to quilt it. The stitches should stop short of the top of each leaf to represent the vein.

4. Stitch the leaves to the stem, pushing them down as close to the body as possible.

Small Pillow Sachet

Cut 2 pattern pieces for the sachet. Stitch as for the pillow. Stuff three-fourths full and fill the rest of the way with a mixture of long-grain rice, ground cloves, cinnamon, and a drop of strawberry oil.

Cut the leaves with pinking shears and draw veins on each leaf with a black ballpoint pen. Do not use markers, as they may bleed on the fabric.

For hanging

Cut a 2½-inch piece of satin or grosgrain ribbon, fold it in half and stitch to the base of the stem. Tack each of the leaves around the stem.

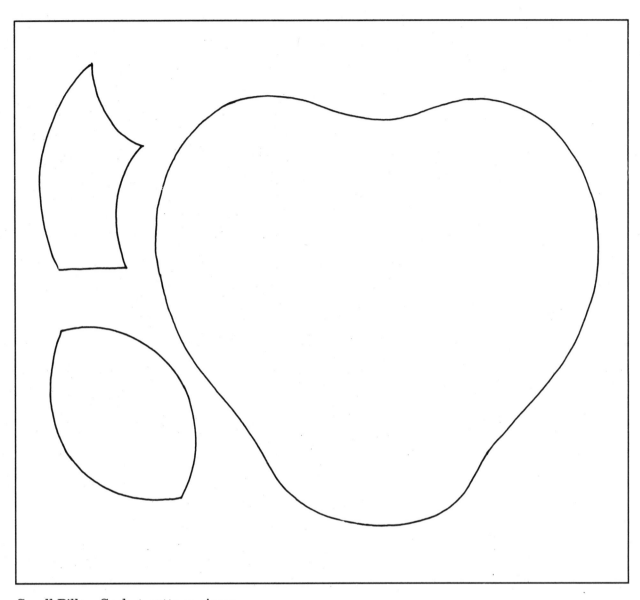

Small Pillow Sachet pattern pieces

Holiday Place Mat

It's always fun to add a little Christmas spirit to your decorating during the holidays. Make a colorful patchwork place mat from all the red and green scraps you have left over from other projects. This makes a good last-minute gift, or bazaar item. If you use scraps it doesn't have to cost you a cent. The finished size is 12 x 16 inches.

Materials (for one place mat)
variety of green and red printed fabric scraps
quilt batting
backing fabric 12 x 16 inches
1 package 1-inch-wide hem facing

Directions
1. Cut all the scrap fabric pieces into 2½-inch squares (includes ¼-inch seam allowance). Arrange the pieces in a pleasing pattern.

2. With right sides facing, stitch 2 patches together along one edge. Open and press the seam. Continue to join patches until you have 8 rows of 6 squares.

3. With right sides facing and edges aligned, join the rows so you have 8 across and 6 down.

4. Cut batting the same size as the place mat top and pin top, batting, and backing together. Machine-stitch to quilt along all seam lines.

To finish

1. Stitch the hem facing ¼ inch in from the raw edge all around the top.

2. Fold to the back and stitch to the back edge ¼ inch in from the raw edge. Press.

Christmas Table Setting

It's easy and fun to set a festive table for the holidays. Make place mats from pretreated artist's canvas, available in art supply stores. The background is faux finished with a sponge glaze technique that's amazingly foolproof, over which a stencil design is applied.

To complete the scene, make a centerpiece with a plain plastic planter given the texture of granite that you simply spray on. Add a pretty bow and fill with a bright red poinsettia. Complete the scene by applying a marble finish to your old wooden, glass, or ceramic candle holders. It's a cinch!

Materials (for 4 place mats)

artist's canvas (each placemat is 12 x 17 inches)

white latex paint

2–3 inch sponge brush

1 pint each dark and clear Formby's Decorative Touches Sponge
  Glaze Mix (available at home centers and craft supply stores)

natural sponge

1 tube each green and red acrylic paint

precut stencil with holiday motif

stencil brush

Formby's Clear Finish

Directions (for place mats)

Rule off and cut the number of placemats needed from the artist's canvas.

Preparing the background:

1. In a throwaway container, mix 1 teaspoon green acrylic paint with 1 cup white latex paint. Stir for a pale green consistency. This is enough to paint 4 place mats with some leftover for your faux finish. If you're crafting 6 to 8 place mats, double the amount of paints.

2. Using the sponge brush, paint the front of each place mat. Let dry.

3. Mix 1 part Formby's dark glaze mix with 3 parts pale green paint mixture. Dip the natural sponge into the glaze mixture and dab excess onto newsprint. Next, dab the sponge over the front of the place mats in a random pattern, turning your hand this way and that as you do this. Continue to create a textured background on each place mat. Set aside to dry. Rinse out the sponge in warm water.

To stencil

1. Add ½ teaspoon of Formby's clear glaze mix to a tablespoon of green acrylic paint and mix.

2. Position the stencil in one corner of the place mat. Dip your stencil brush into the paint/glaze mixture and dab off excess onto newsprint.

3. While holding the stencil firmly in position with one hand, use the other to dab the green glaze onto the cutout leaves of the design.

4. Repeat on all place mats. Remove stencil and let the paint dry.

Rinse the stencil brush in warm water until it runs clear. You are now ready for the second color.

5. Mix the red acrylic with the clear glaze as you did for the green color. Holding the stencil in position, fill in the flower cutout areas with the red paint/glaze mixture. Repeat on all place mats. Let dry.

To finish

1. Protect the front of each place mat with Formby's Clear Finish.

2. Let dry and recoat if desired. Your place mats can be cleaned after each use with a slightly damp, regular sponge.

Materials (for plant holder and candle holders)

1 plastic plant holder

2 glass, ceramic, metal, or wooden candle holders

1 aerosol can each Formby's Decorative Touches Granite Finish Midnight Stars), Marble Base Finish (green) and Marble Highlight (gold)

Formby's Clear Finish

1 yard satin ribbon

glue gun or craft glue

Directions

1. Follow directions on the can and spray entire planter with the Granite Finish. Set aside to dry.

2. Follow directions on the can and spray the candlesticks with the Marble Base. Let dry.

3. Before applying the Marble Highlight to the candle holders, practice on a scrap board or paper to get the feeling for creating the look of marble veins. You might even look at real marble or a picture of a marble object for inspiration. Then apply the marble highlight in short, sweeping bursts over the green base of the candlesticks. This is so much fun and the results are so good that you'll probably want to faux finish a variety of objects. For example, you can finish several holders in different colors.

4. Protect candle holders and planter with Formby's Clear Finish. Let dry.

5. Tie satin ribbon into a fat bow and glue to the front of the plant holder.

6. Insert plant.

Materials (for decoupage plates)
clear glass plates
paper illustration (from wrapping paper, book, print, etc.)
small scissors
white craft glue
1 each of Formby's Decorative Touches Marble Base Finish
    (color of you choice), Marble Highlight (gold or silver).
    Formby's Clear Finish

Directions

1. Cut out illustration.
2. Apply white glue to front of illustration and glue to the underside of the plate. Smooth out until all traces of glue are transparent. Use a damp sponge to wipe away excess glue. Let dry completely (2 hours).
3. Apply gold Marble Highlight in a short sweeping motion across the back of the plate. Let dry.
4. Next, apply green Base Finish to the back of the plate. Let dry.
5. Apply Clear Finish over the Base Finish and let dry completely. Repeat several times to protect the finish.
6. Do not use these plates for serving food, but rather as a decorative element. To clean, use a damp sponge on the front of the glass dish.

Christmas Patch Pillow

This Christmas wreath patchwork pillow will be most appreciated for holiday spruce-up in any home. You can make it with white and green printed fabric. The center is made with red Aida even-weave fabric so you can cross-stitch the message on it. (See page 20 for easy cross-stitch directions.) The finished size is 14 x 14 inches.

Materials
½ yard fabric A
½ yard fabric B
6½-inch square of red 12-count Aida cloth
1 skein white embroidery floss
embroidery hoop
needle
solid fabric for backing
Poly-Fil stuffing
½ yard of 2-inch-wide red ribbon

Directions
Cut 2 6½-inch squares from fabric A. Cut 2 6½-inch squares from fabric B. Fold all fabric squares on the diagonal and cut on the line. You now have 4 triangles of each fabric.

Refer to the piecing diagram and with right sides facing stitch A and B triangles together with ½-inch seam allowance. Press all seams on back of patched piece.

To cross-stitch
Center letters on Aida cloth and follow chart to do cross-stitch. (See general directions on page 20.)

To finish
Place patched piece over red Aida and adjust so the word is centered. Pin in place and stitch around edge by hand or on the machine with same color thread.

Use this as your pattern for the back and pin to backing fabric. Cut around outside edge. If you want to add piping to the outside edge, see page 21 for complete directions.

With right sides facing, stitch around all edges with a ½-inch seam allowance. Leave one side of octagonal shape open for turning. Turn to right side and stuff with Poly-Fil. Close top with slip-stitch.

Make a ribbon bow and tack to top of pillow.

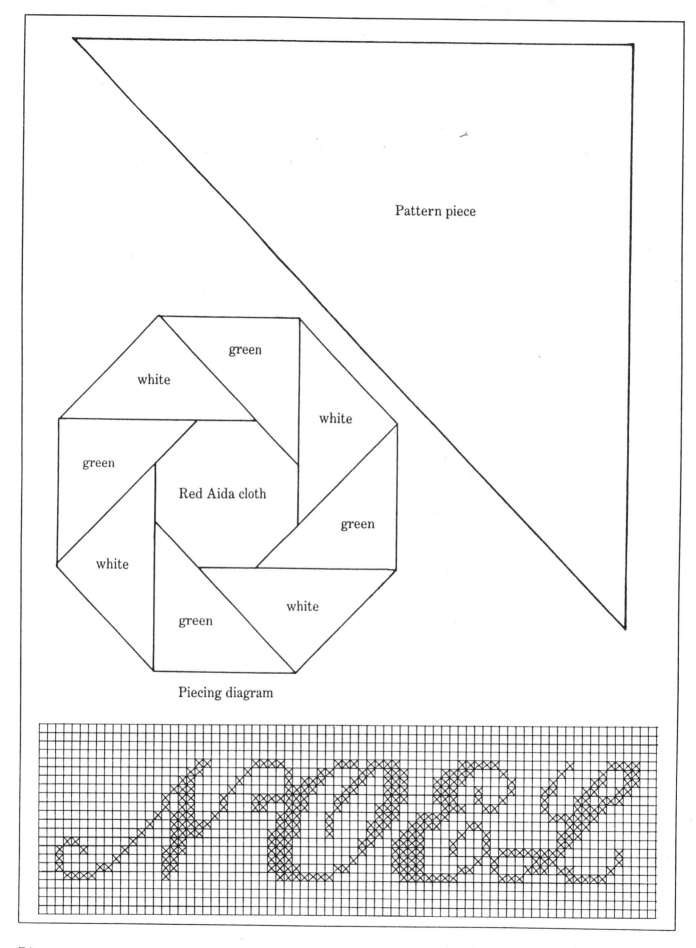

Pattern piece

green

white

white

green

Red Aida cloth

green

white

white

green

Piecing diagram

Personal Gifts

Christmas Coasters

It's always a treat to bring out accessories that are used only at Christmastime. They cheer up the house and make it special when entertaining. So while these coasters probably won't be used at any other time of the year, they are very cheery for that special time. Choose alphabet letters from pages 77 and 78 and make one with a friend's first initial and another with the last.

Materials
10-count plastic canvas, 4½-inch square (if precut)
1-2-3 ply Persian-type yarn:
     1 skein each of red and green, 2 skeins white
needle
red or green felt for backing
glue

Directions
1. Use the Continental stitch and follow the chart for placement of colors. When finished, bind off with a row of green worked around the edge and into last row worked with green.
2. Cut a square of felt for back of each coaster and glue or stitch in place.

□ white

☒ red

▣ green

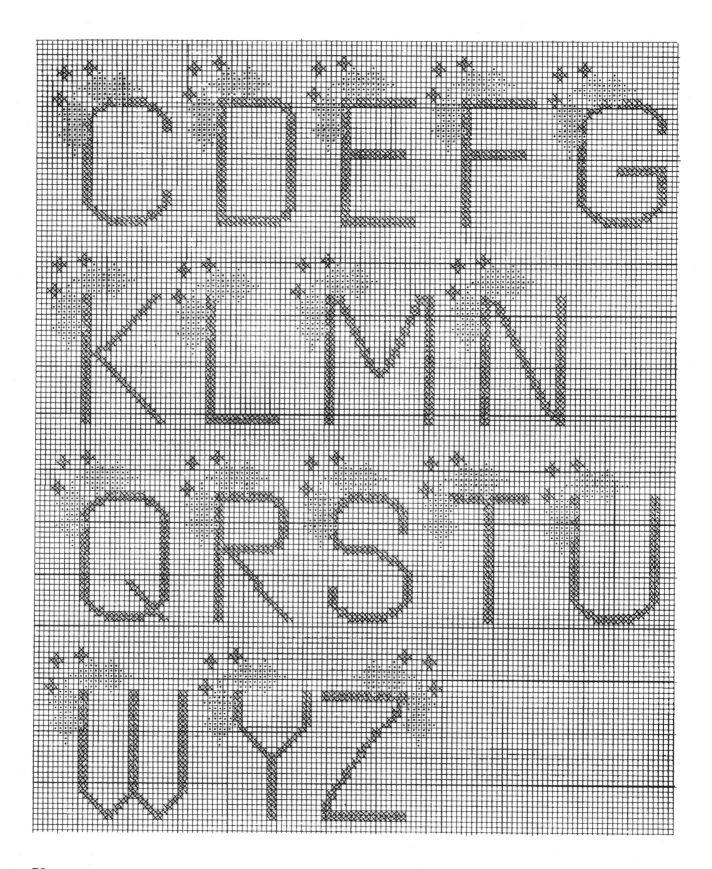

78

Clutch Purse

This would be a nice gift for your mother or a personal friend. Pick a delicate floral, overall print for a clutch purse or lingerie case. The finished size is 9 x 13 inches, which is quite roomy. The lining is a bright, contrasting solid color. The blue lines on the fabric are the stitches that accent and quilt the fabric. Originally, hand embroidery was often used as a quilting technique when a decorative finish was preferred.

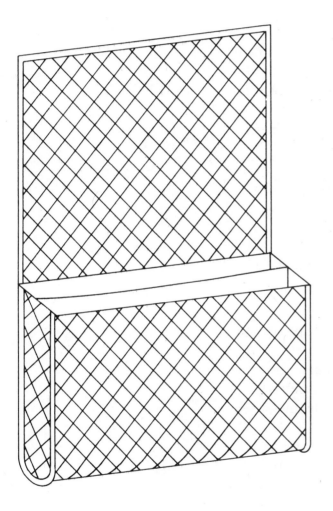

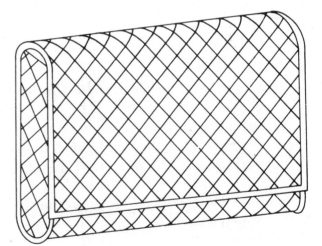

Materials

½ yard 45-inch-wide printed fabric
½ yard (any width) solid fabric
quilt batting
thread to match fabric
needle
tracing paper
ruler
hard pencil
button or snap for closure

Directions

All directions include a ¼-inch seam allowance.

1. Begin by tracing pattern piece A. This is the pattern for the sides of the bag.

2. Pin the pattern to the printed fabric and cut two. Repeat for lining fabric.

3. From the printed fabric, cut pieces in the following sizes:

    14 x 27½ inches for main piece
    10½ x 14 inches for flap lining

4. From solid fabric, cut pieces in the following sizes:

    7½ x 12¾ inches for pocket
    12¾ x 16 inches for main lining piece

5. Cut batting 14 x 27½ inches.

6. Cut 2 pieces of batting, using pattern piece A as a guide. Cut away seam allowance.

To quilt

1. Use a ruler to mark off a grid over the main fabric piece (14 x 27½ inches).

2. Pin batting to the back of the main piece and machine-stitch along all drawn lines, stopping ¼ inch from the fabric's edge.

3. Rule off lines on the flap lining fabric and machine-stitch without batting.

4. Rule off lines on the side pieces (A) and pin to the corresponding batting pieces.

5. Stitch along all marked lines.

To assemble

1. Place the main fabric piece right-side up, lengthwise, on your work table.

2. With right sides facing and raw edges aligned, pin the flap lining piece to one short end of the main piece.

Tissue Box Cover

A small project like this is easy to make for gift giving, bazaar sales, or to pretty up your own bath or bedroom.

An overall small print is a good choice for quilting in a grid pattern. Quilting is an option, but it makes the project more elegant. Use a contrasting piping for added interest.

Materials
¼ yard calico fabric
thin quilt batting
1 yard piping in color to match
embroidery floss to match a color in the fabric
quilting needle
tissue box

Directions
The tissue box is used as your template for measuring fabric pieces. You can use these directions for making a cover for any size box, the only variable being the amount of fabric used.

1. Begin by cutting 1 piece of fabric to fit the top of the box, adding ½ inch all around.

2. Measure the perimeter and height of the box and cut 1 strip of fabric to these dimensions, adding ½ inch all around. This piece wraps around the four sides of the box.

3. Cut a piece of batting ½ inch smaller all around for each piece of fabric.

4. If there are no guidelines, such as stripes, checks, or a grid on your fabric print, rule off evenly spaced horizontal and vertical lines, using a ruler and hard pencil or water soluble marker.

5. Pin the corresponding batting piece to the wrong side of each fabric piece.

6. Remove the top opening piece from the tissue box. Using this as your template, center it on the top fabric piece with the batting and mark around it with a pencil (Figure 1).

7. Working ½ inch inside the lines you just drew, refer to Figure 2 and cut out an opening on the fabric and batting. Notch curved edges.

8. Cut a piece of fabric on the bias, 1 inch wide and long enough to fit around the opening plus an extra ½ inch. Turn the long edges under ¼ inch and press. Turn 1 short end under ½ inch and press. Fold the strip in half lengthwise and press.

9. Encase the raw edge of the opening in the bias strip, overlapping the edges where they meet. Stitch around.

To quilt

Using embroidery thread in a contrasting or matching color, separate all 6 strands. Using 3 strands only, quilt along the premarked lines, using a back or running stitch (page 15). An alternative way to quilt the fabric is on the machine, using a matching thread on the fabric. In this way you will have a quilted project without the emphasis on the decorative stitching. If you enjoy lap work, you can simply quilt the fabric with small running stitches as one might do for a quilt.

1. Begin on the back of each panel. Make a small knot and pull the thread through the batting and fabric. Try to keep your stitches even and taut without bunching the fabric as you sew.

2. If stitching on the machine, set the stitch-length dial for a longer stitch than the one you would use for regular seam stitching, but not as loose as for a basting stitch. Do not allow stitching to run into the seam allowance.

To assemble

1. With right sides facing and raw edges aligned, join the short ends of the side piece, leaving a ½-inch seam allowance.

2. With raw edges aligned, pin the piping around the outer edge of the top piece of fabric. Stitch around.

3. With right sides facing and piping between, pin and join the top and side sections (Figure 3).

4. Trim all seam allowances as close to the stitching line as possible. Turn right-side out and slip over the tissue box.

5. Pull the cover down so it fits comfortably over the box and turn the raw edge under ¼ inch all around the bottom of the cover. Pin in place.

6. Remove the cover and stitch around the bottom edge. Replace on the tissue box.

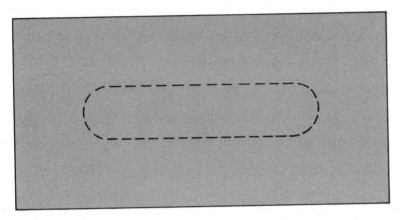

Figure 1

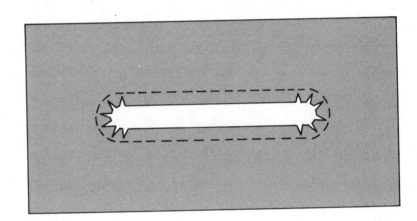

Figure 2

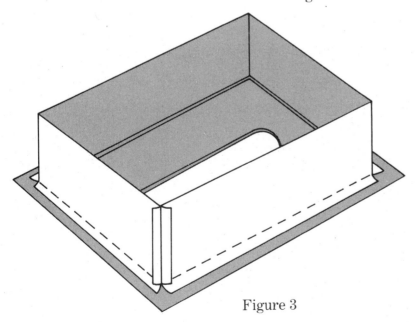

Figure 3

Eyeglass Case

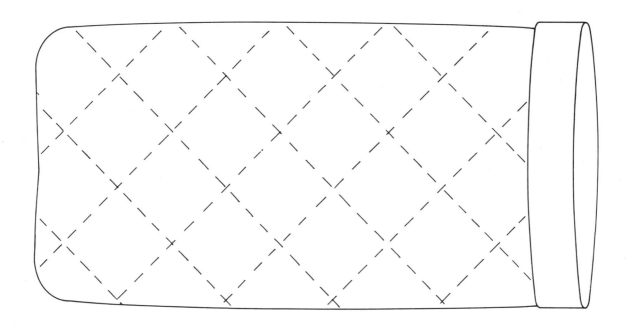

A tiny, overall, delicate rosebud print is perfect for an eyeglass case. The lines are done with embroidery stitches in order to quilt the fabric and add this delightful decorative touch.

Materials

7 x 14½ inches delicate print fabric
7 x 14½ inches solid fabric (bright red used here)
7 inches decorative braid (green)
6½ x 14 inches thin quilt batting
1 skein embroidery floss (red)
embroidery needle

Directions

1. Cut printed outside fabric and solid lining in half so you have 4 pieces of fabric, 3½ x 7¼ inches each.
2. Cut batting in half so you have 2 pieces 6¼ x 7 inches.
3. Pin both outside fabric pieces to the batting pieces.
4. Draw a grid across the fabric, between the floral pattern, using a light pencil.
5. Using 3 strands of the embroidery floss, take small running stitches along all marked lines through the fabric and batting on both pieces of fabric.
6. With right sides facing, stitch front and back quilted fabric together along side and bottom edges, leaving the top edge open. Turn.

Lining

1. With right sides facing and raw edges aligned, stitch the 2 lining pieces together with ⅜-inch seam allowance along the side and bottom edges. Leave the top edge open. (The lining should be slightly smaller in order to fit comfortably inside the case.)

2. Trim seams and clip corners, but do not turn right-side out.

3. Slip lining inside the quilted case and smooth into position.

4. Make sure that the side seams line up and tack the lining in position at the bottom corners.

To finish

1. Turn the top raw edges of the outside case and the lining ¼ inch to the inside (between outside and lining) and press.

2. Pin the decorative braid or ribbon around the top edge.

3. Slipstitch braid and top edge of fabric and lining all around. Slipstitch bottom edge of braid to top fabric only.

Bookmarks

Bookmarks are quick little projects that I've designed to be whimsical for a change of pace. There is a bee and flower on one, a boat and anchor on another, a cat and mouse that you can make for a child, and a monogram with hearts.

Give someone you care about a book for Christmas and add your handmade gift for that special touch.

Materials (for each bookmark)
Small amount of 10-count plastic canvas
1-2-3 ply Persian yarn in the colors indicated on each chart
¼-inch-wide satin ribbon, 10 inches long
needle

Directions
The Continental stitch is used for all projects (page 15). Start with a big enough canvas so you can work the pattern with plenty of room all around it. Follow the chart for each design and use the colors on the key.

When finished with each piece, cut out shape in the middle of the row next to the last finished row. Bind off around cut edges and through last worked rows.

Cut ribbon lengths approximately 10 inches long and stitch each end to the 2 parts of the design. One piece is inserted in the book, the other hangs out above the pages.

When working on the monogram project, refer to page 91 for alphabet letters.

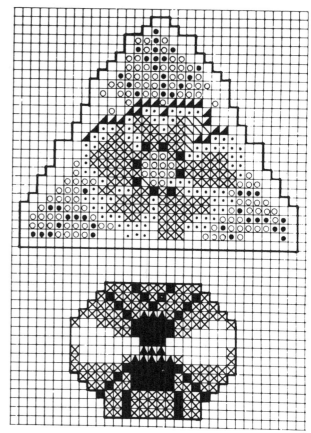

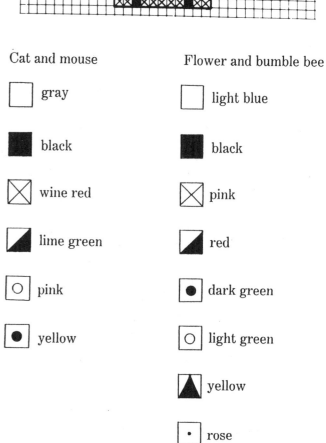

Cat and mouse

☐ gray

■ black

⊠ wine red

◪ lime green

○ pink

● yellow

Flower and bumble bee

☐ light blue

■ black

⊠ pink

◪ red

● dark green

○ light green

▲ yellow

· rose

90

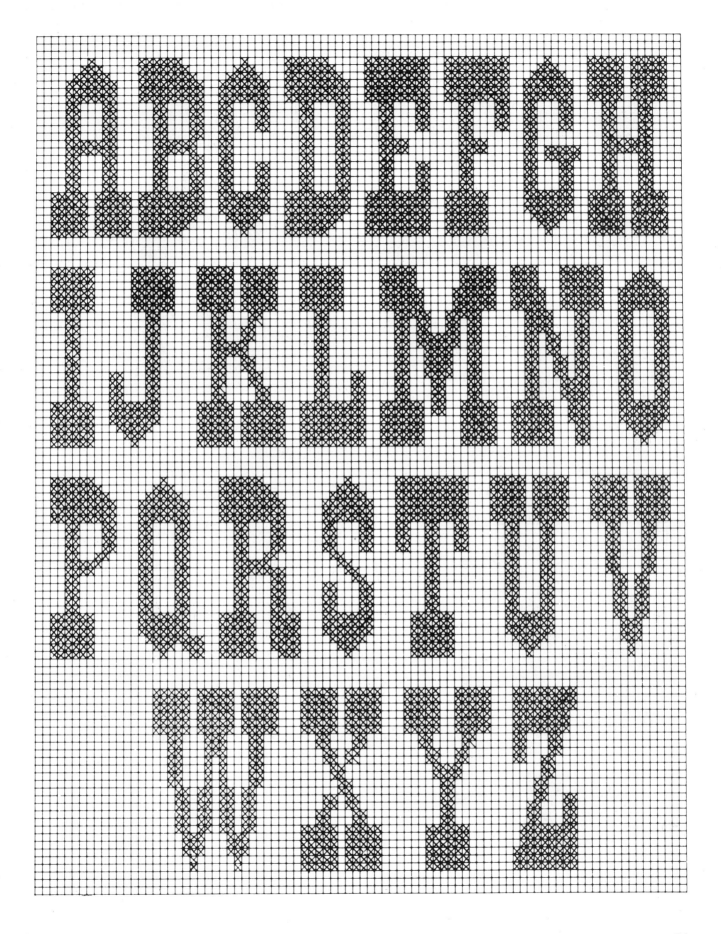

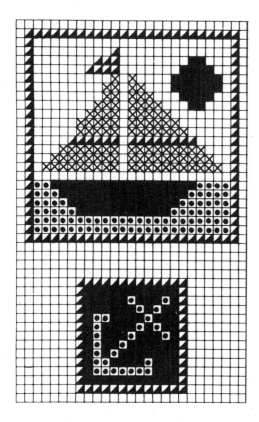

Sailboat and anchor

☐ light blue

■ yellow

⊠ white

◸ red

⊡ medium blue

Monogram bookmark

⊠ wine red

⊡ pink

☐ white

Gifts for Children

Beanbag Toys: Frog, Octopus, Juggling Balls, Santa Claus

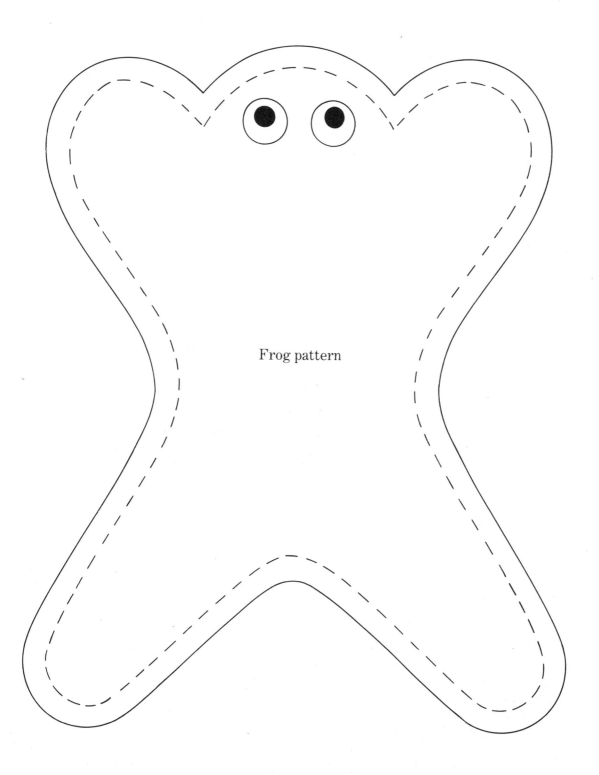

Frog pattern

This is a popular bazaar item for young children as well as teenagers. The frogs have googly eyes and are silly-looking. The octopus is right at home with his "legs" straddling a shelf. Santa is fun all year long, and the juggling balls will delight young and old alike.

Frog

Materials
piece of green calico 6 x 8 inches
piece of blue fabric 6 x 8 inches
2 white pom-poms
scrap of black felt
white glue
beans, seeds, peas, or corn for filling
tracing paper

Directions
The pattern piece for cutting fabric includes a ¼-inch seam allowance.
1. Trace the frog pattern from this book.
2. Cut one piece from green fabric and one from the blue.
3. With right sides facing and raw edges aligned, pin the green and blue fabrics together. Stitch around, leaving a small opening at the mouth for turning and filling.
4. Trim around seams and clip around curves. Turn right-side out and press.
5. Fill the frog two-thirds full. Do not stitch opening closed until you have stitched the eyes in place so you can reach in to hold your needle on the underside of the top fabric.
6. Stitch pom-pom eyes on top of the calico head. Cut small circles of black felt and glue them on the white eyeballs.
7. Turn raw edges under and slip-stitch opening closed.

Octopus

Materials
small amount of blue calico
small amount of peach calico
beans, seeds, peas, or corn for filling
2 white pom-poms or moveable eyes
tracing paper
stiff paper

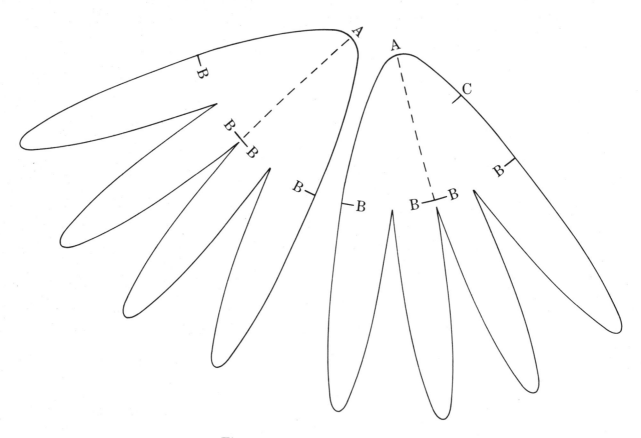

Figure 1. Assembling top pieces

Figure 2. Underbody assembly

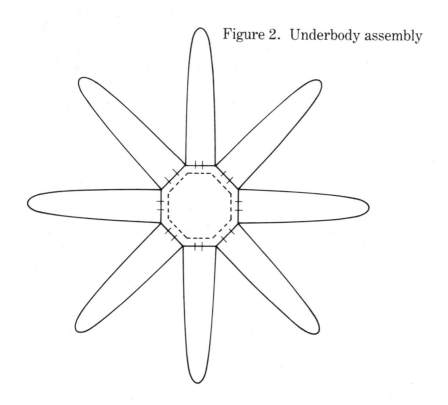

Braided Wreath: page 31

Cookie Cutter Ornaments: page 132

Sleepy-Time Doll Stocking: page 120

Noel Banner: page 24

Around-the-World Quilt: page 38

Elf Stocking: page 117

Patchwork Stocking and Ornament: page 114

Basket Full of Strawberries: page 61

No-Sew Apple Collage: page 48

Pinwheel Pillows: page 103

Festive Fabric Frame: page 58

Holiday Place Mat: page 66

Calico Tree Treasures: page 151

Santa Stocking and Ornaments: page 127

Christmas Lap Quilt: page 52

Babes-in-Toyland Stocking: page 124

Babes-in-Toyland Ornaments: page 125

Christmas Patch Pillow: page 72

Bookmarks: page 88

Bookmarks: page 88

Mini-Stocking Ornaments: page 155

Clutch Purse: page 79; Tissue Box Cover: page 83; Eyeglass Case: page 86

Calico Teacup Wallhanging: page 33

Heart-Warming Hearts: page 148

Ribbon Stars: page 146

Christmas Coasters: page 76

Christmas Table Setting: page 68

Gingham Baby Quilt: page 108

Beanbag Toys: page 94

Angel Cat: page 139

Cool Cats: page 141

Christmas Star Wallhanging: page 42

Three Bears: page 135

Magical Mystical Stars and Moon: page 143

Octopus patterns

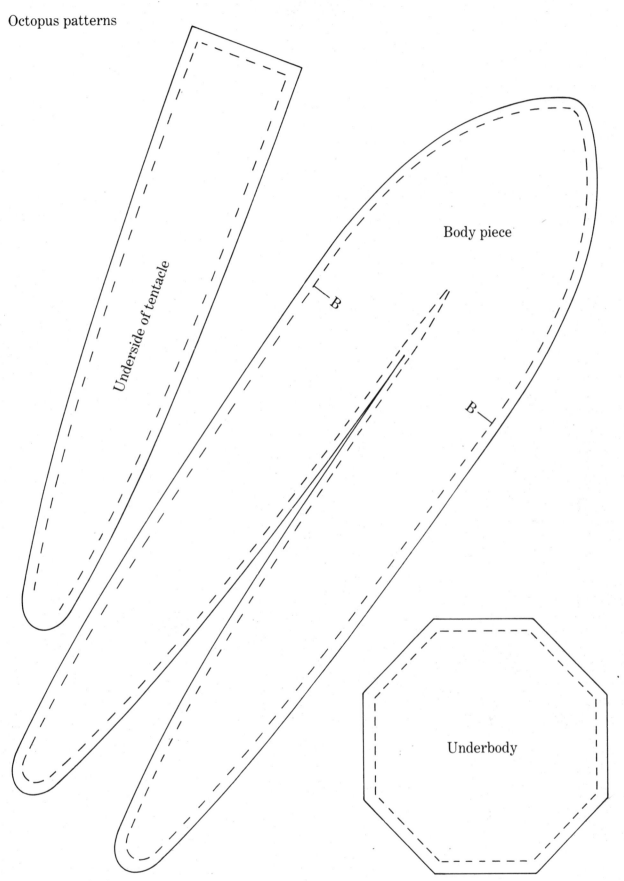

Underside of tentacle

Body piece

B

B

Underbody

Note: ⅛-inch seam allowance

Directions

The body is 9 inches around and each tentacle is 6 inches long. The pattern includes a ¼-inch seam allowance.

1. Trace the patterns and transfer to stiff paper for a template (page 16).
2. Using the template, draw around the body on the wrong side of the blue calico 4 times.
3. Using the template for the underside of the tentacles, draw 8 on the wrong side of the peach calico.
4. Using the underbody pattern, draw one on the wrong side of the peach calico.
5. Cut out all pieces.
6. With right sides facing and raw edges aligned, pin 2 body pieces together and stitch down one side from point A to point B on broken line, as shown in Figure 1.
7. Repeat with the other 2 body pieces.
8. With right sides facing and raw edges aligned, pin the 2 top pieces together. Stitch from the left-hand point B up over the top past point A to C, leaving and opening from C to the right-hand point B and continuing down to the edge of the tentacle.

Lining

1. With right sides facing and raw edges aligned, pin the 8 peach tentacles to the underbody piece (Figure 2). Stitch around.
2. With right sides facing and raw edges aligned, pin the underbody and tentacle lining to the head and tentacles, matching the bases of the tentacles. Stitch around all tentacles.
3. Clip curves between tentacles. Cut across the tips of each tentacle close to the seams.
4. Turn the octopus right-side out and fill with beans.
5. Turn raw edges under and slip-stitch opening closed.
6. Stitch 2 pom-pom eyes in place on front of face.

Juggling Balls

Materials (for 3 balls)
small amounts of red, blue, green, and yellow calico
small beans for filling
tracing paper
stiff paper

Directions
This is a very easy project to make from 2 pieces of fabric, one

pattern, and a continuous seam. Each ball is 9½ inches around. The pattern includes a ¼-inch seam allowance.

1. Trace the pattern and transfer to stiff paper for a template (page 16).
2. Place the template on the wrong side of the fabric and draw around once on the red, blue, and green calico. Make 3 on yellow fabric.
3. Cut out all fabric pieces.
4. With right sides facing and raw edges aligned, pin a yellow piece to the red piece, matching the end marks on the yellow with the center marks on the red, and the end marks on the red to the center marks on the yellow.
5. Repeat, using a yellow piece and the blue piece.
6. Repeat, using a yellow piece and the green piece.
7. Stitch a continuous seam all around each ball, leaving a small opening for turning and filling.
8. Turn right-side out and fill with small beans. Turn raw edges under and slip-stitch opening closed.

Santa

Materials
small scraps of red, green, blue, and pink calico
small beans for filling
3 yards white yarn
embroidery needle
2 tiny moveable eyes or black felt
white glue
pom-pom for nose
tracing paper
fusible webbing

Directions
All patterns include a ¼-inch seam allowance. The Santa beanbag is 15 inches tall.

1. Trace the pattern pieces from these pages.
2. Fold the red calico in half and cut out the body and hat.
3. Fold the pink fabric in half and cut out the face pattern.
4. Cut 2 green boots. Turn pattern over and cut 2 more.
5. Cut 2 gloves, toes, and heels from the blue fabric. Turn patterns over and cut 2 more of each.
6. With right sides facing and raw edges aligned, stitch the hat

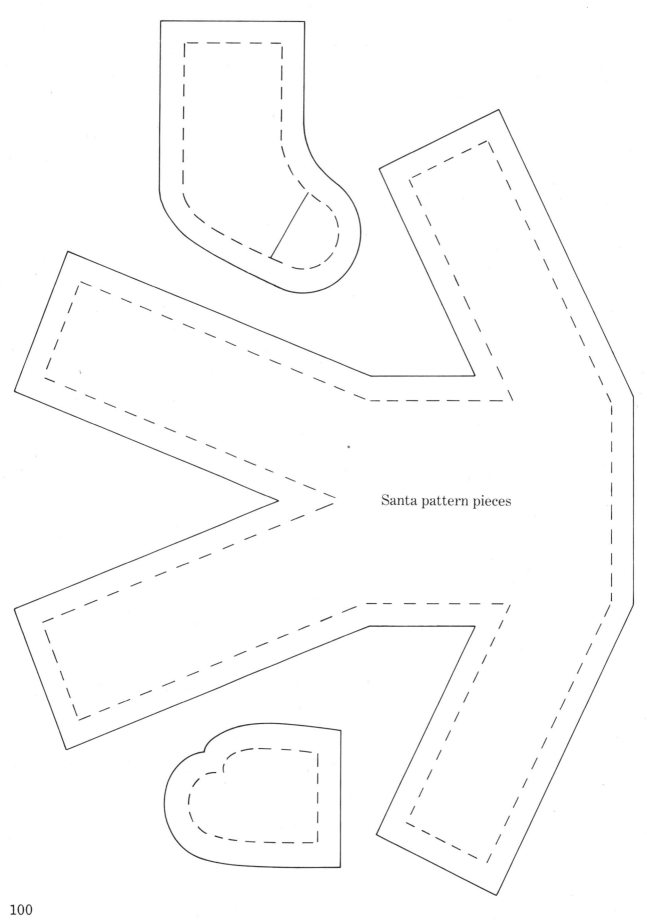

Santa pattern pieces

pieces to the face pieces along the top edge of the face.

7. Join face pieces to the body pieces at the neck in the same way.

8. Next, join the glove pieces to the arms, and boot pieces to the legs. Open all seams and press.

9. Cut a piece of fusible webbing for the heel and toe pieces and position fabric and webbing on boot. Fuse with a medium-hot iron.

10. With right sides facing and raw edges aligned, pin Santa's front and back together and stitch around, leaving a small opening in the side of the hat for turning and filling.

11. Turn right-side out and fill.

12. Turn raw edges under and slip-stitch opening closed.

To finish

1. Glue moveable eyes in place on face.

2. Stitch nose in center of face.

3. Using the embroidery needle and white yarn, make big loops around face for beard.

4. Add a pom-pom tassel to the top of Santa's hat.

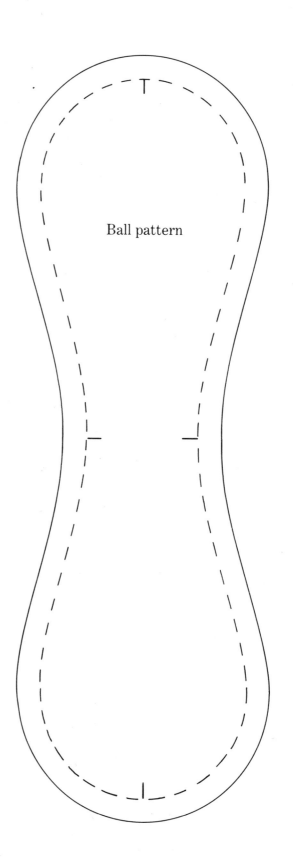

Ball pattern

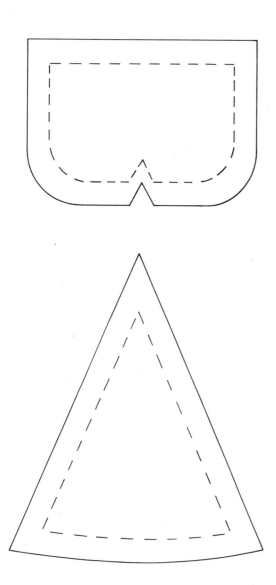

Santa pattern pieces

Pinwheel Pillows

These Pinwheel pillows are perfect small quilting projects. Use fabric with pastel colors or those with a bright holiday theme. The finished size is 12 x 12 inches and can be filled with stuffing or a standard pillow form.

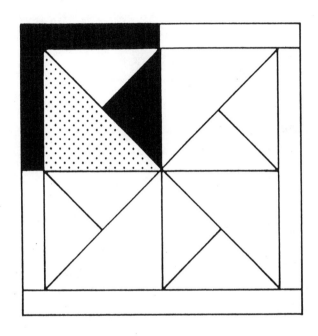

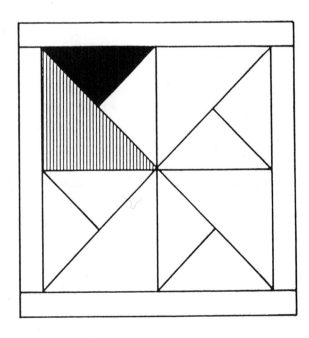

Materials (for 2 pillows)
½ yard peach fabric
½ yard blue fabric
⅓ yard green fabric
⅓ yard yellow fabric
½ yard quilt batting
12 x 12-inch pillow forms or stuffing
49 inches cording for each pillow
tracing paper
cardboard for template

Directions

All measurements include ¼-inch seam allowance. Trace and transfer pattern pieces A and B to cardboard to make templates (see page 16). Cut out.

Pillow 1

Using the templates, cut the following from green
    A: 4
from yellow
    borders: 2 strips, each 1½ x 10½ inches
              2 strips, each 1½ x 12½ inches
    B: 4
from peach
    backing piece 12½ x 12½ inches
    B: 4

To assemble

Refer to Figure 1.

1. With right sides facing and raw edges aligned, join a yellow B piece to a peach B piece along one short edge to make a large triangle as shown.
2. Press seam to one side.
3. Repeat with the remaining yellow B and peach B pieces.
4. With right sides facing and long edges aligned, join all yellow/peach triangles to the green triangle A pieces. Press seams to one side.
5. Refer to Figure 2 to join all 4 squares, making a small pinwheel in the center of the pillow top. Press seams to one side.
6. Next, add the borders in the following way. With right sides facing and raw edges aligned, attach a yellow 1½ x 10½-inch strip to one side edge of the block. Press seam to one side. Repeat

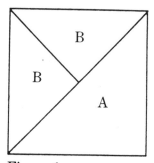

Figure 1

on the opposite side.

7. Join the long strips to the top and bottom edges in the same way to complete the pillow top.

To quilt

1. Cut the quilt batting 11½ x 11½ inches and pin to the back of the pillow top.

2. Taking small running stitches, quilt ¼ inch from each side of all seam lines.

3. To make piping, refer to page 21.

4. With raw edges matching, pin piping around the edge of the pillow top, overlapping the ends.

5. Stitch the piping to the pillow top as close to the cording as possible.

6. With right sides facing and raw edges aligned, stitch the backing piece to the pillow top, using the piping stitches as a guide and leaving 8 inches across one edge open for turning. Trim seams and clip corners.

7. Turn right-side out and insert soft pillow form or stuffing. Slip-stitch opening closed or insert a zipper according to package directions.

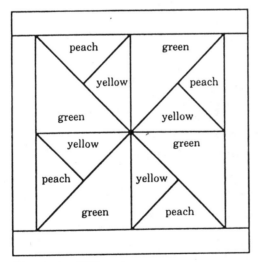

Figure 2. Pillow 1

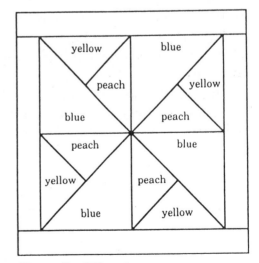

Figure 3. Pillow 2

Pillow 2

Use the same templates and cut the following
from blue
       backing piece 12½ x 12½ inches
       A: 4
from yellow
       B: 4
from peach
       borders: 2 strips, each 1½ x 10½ inches
              2 strips, each 1½ x 12½ inches
       B: 4

Follow directions for pillow 1 and refer to Figure 3.

To finish

1. Use any one of the fabrics to make a strip of fabric 1½ x 50 inches long for the piping to go around the pillow top. To do this, cut shorter strips of fabric on the bias and stitch the short ends of the strips together to make one long strip.

2. Beginning ½ inch from the end of the fabric, place the cording in the center of the wrong side of the fabric. Fold the fabric over the cording so the raw edges of the fabric meet.

3. Use a zipper foot on your sewing machine and stitch as close to the cording as possible to encase it in the fabric.

4. With right sides facing and raw edges aligned, pin the piping around the edge of the pillow top, overlapping the ends.

5. Stitch the piping to the pillow top as close to the cording as possible.

6. With right sides facing and raw edges aligned, stitch the backing piece to the pillow top, using the piping stitches as a guide and leaving 8 inches across one edge open for turning. Trim seams and clip corners.

7. Turn right-side out and insert pillow form or stuffing. Slip-stitch opening closed or insert zipper according to package directions.

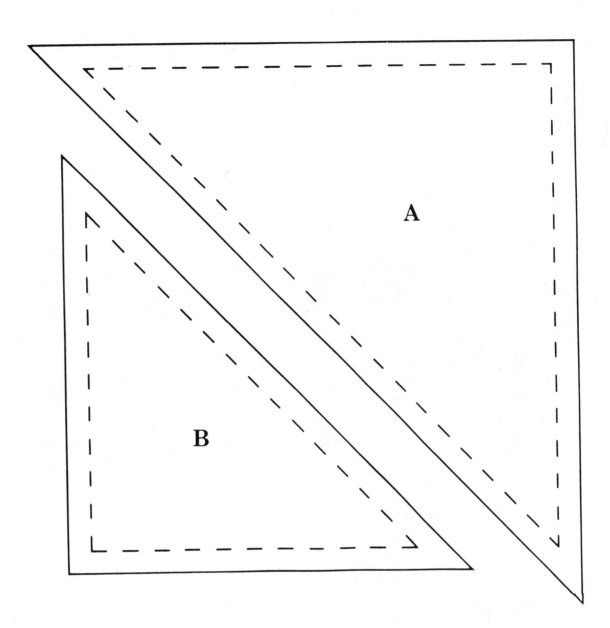

A

B

Gingham Baby Quilt

This baby coverlet, made from different gingham fabric colors, is easy and expandable. Since it is made up of squares, you can make it to fit a carriage, crib, or youth bed. You can use any fabrics, solid or printed, in delicate colors. By using only 9 squares, you can make a pillow cover to match. This is a wonderful weekend project. The finished size is 39 x 39 inches and will fit a crib.

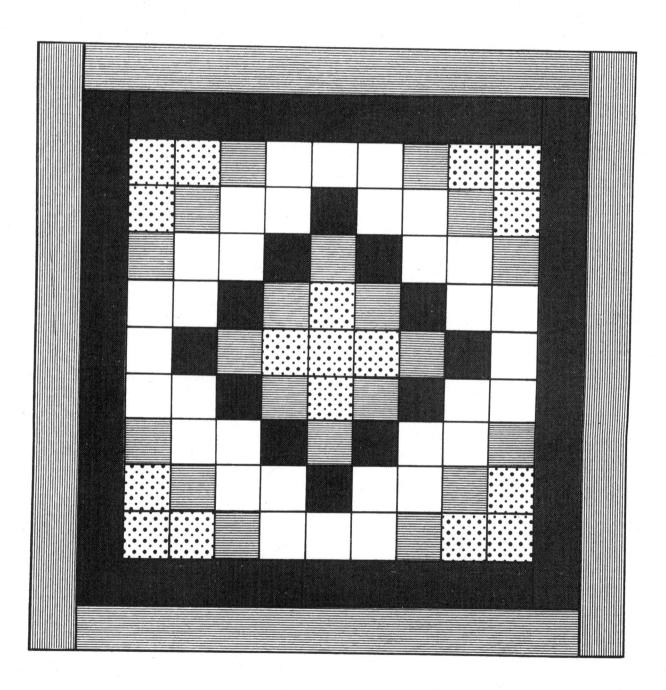

Materials (all fabric is 45 inches wide)
½ yard yellow gingham A
1 yard pink gingham B
1 yard blue gingham C
½ yard white fabric D
1½ yards backing fabric
batting
thread to match fabric colors
needle for hand-quilting

Directions

Cut the following border pieces:
B — 2 pieces 3½ x 33½ inches for top and bottom
B — 2 pieces 3½ x 39½ inches for the sides
C — 2 pieces 3½ x 27½ inches for top and bottom
C — 2 pieces 3½ x 33½ inches for the sides
Cut the following number of squares 3½ x 3½ inches:
A — 17 squares
B — 20 squares
C — 12 squares
D — 32 squares

To make a row

1. With right sides facing and raw edges aligned, stitch 2 A squares together along one side.
2. Open seams and press.
3. Refer to Figure 1 and join a B square, followed by 3 D squares, then a B square, followed by 2 A squares, for a total of 9 squares in the row.
4. Open all seams and press.
5. Continue with 8 more rows. The following is the pattern sequence:

Figure 1

| A | A | B | D | D | D | B | A | A |

| A | A | B | D | D | D | B | A | A |

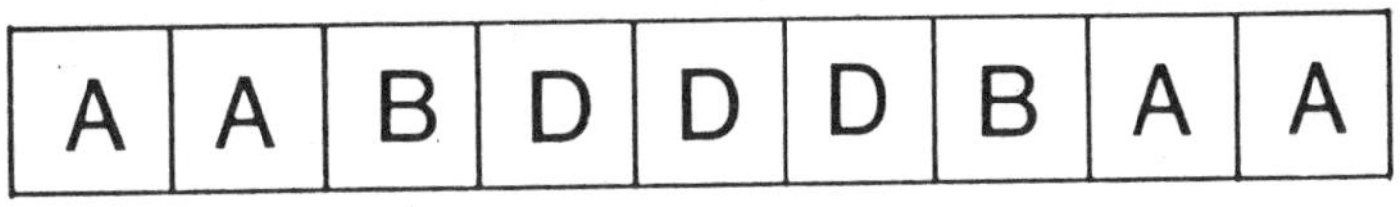

Row 2: A-B-D-D-C-D-D-B-A

Row 3: B-D-D-C-B-C-D-D-B

Row 4: D-D-C-B-A-B-C-D-D

Row 5: D-C-B-A-A-A-B-C-D

Row 6: D-D-C-B-A-B-C-D-D

Row 7: B-D-D-C-B-C-D-D-B

Row 8: A-B-D-D-C-D-D-B-A

Row 9: A-A-B-D-D-D-B-A-A

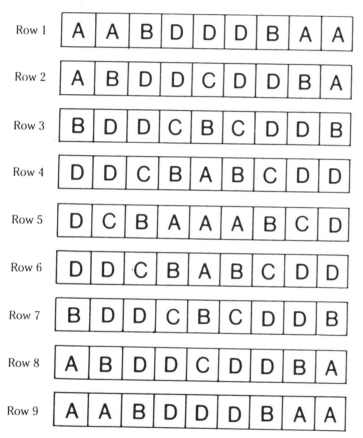

Figure 2

Joining rows

1. With right sides facing and raw edges aligned, join row 1 with row 2 along the bottom long edge.

2. Open seams and press.

3. Refer to Figure 2 and continue to join rows in the same way.

4. Open all seams and press.

Joining borders

1. With right sides facing and raw edges aligned, stitch the top and bottom C border strips to the top and bottom of the quilt top (Figure 3).
2. Open seams and press.
3. Join side C border strips in the same way.
4. Next join the top and bottom B border strips to the top and bottom of the quilt top.
5. Open seams and press.
6. Join side B border strips in the same way.
7. Open all seams and press.

Figure 3

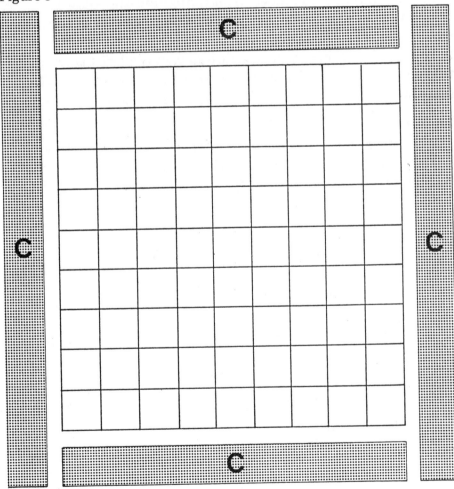

Preparing the backing

1. Cut the batting ½ inch smaller than the quilt top all around.
2. Baste the quilt top and the batting together with long loose stitches.
3. Pin the backing to the front of the quilt top and stitch around 3 sides and 4 corners, leaving 12 inches open on one edge for turning.
4. Clip corners and trim edges close to the seam line.
5. Turn the quilt right-side out so that the batting is between the quilt top and backing fabric.
6. Press all around the edges.

Quilting

1. To hand-quilt, begin at the center of the top and work outward, taking small running stitches ¼ inch on either side of each seam line.
2. To quilt by machine, baste the three layers of fabric together to keep the batting and backing from bunching. Stitch along all seam lines of each gingham square and along the border seams.

To finish

1. When all quilting is complete, clip the basting stitches away.
2. Press the quilt and turn the opening edge of the top and backing to the inside ¼ inch. Press.
3. Slip-stitch opening closed.

Christmas Stockings

Patchwork Stocking and Ornament

Gather all your scrap pieces of fabric together to make a brightly colored Christmas stocking from odds and ends. And then with the smallest pieces you can make a little stocking ornament to fill with candy canes or to hang by the fireplace for the family pet.

Materials (for patchwork stocking)
97 squares of a variety of fabrics, 1½ x 1½ inches
1½ yards eyelet or lace
1½ yards ¼-inch satin ribbon
1½ yards ½-inch grosgrain ribbon
backing fabric (such as felt or printed cotton), 9½ x 14 ½ inches

Directions
Begin by enlarging the stocking pattern (see page 16).
1. To make the patchwork design, cut fabric pieces into 1½ x 1½-inch squares. Select a variety of fabrics that will look good together. For a country classic, choose calico or bright Christmas

material. If you are using two or three different fabrics, cut equal amounts of each. There are so many variations you can create for this project that I'm sure you'll want to take the time to decide what color scheme you'd like best.

2. Follow the diagram (page 116) and sew vertical rows together with ½-inch seam allowance in the following way: 2 rows of 13 squares, 4 rows of 14 squares each, 1 row of 6, 2 rows of 5.

3. Beginning with the heel side, place row 2 on top of row 1 with right sides facing and raw edges aligned. Stitch together on right-hand edge. Open flat and press.

4. Continue to stitch rows together in this way. When all 9 rows are joined, you can cut out stocking shape.

To make stocking

1. Place tracing pattern over patch pieces and pin. Cut out stocking shape. Cut another stocking from the backing material. There will be a ½-inch seam allowance all around.

2. With right sides facing and raw edges aligned, pin eyelet around outside edge of patched piece beginning at top of left edge and ending on opposite side. Do not extend lace across top. Machine-baste.

3. With right sides facing, pin backing to front of stocking and stitch together leaving top open.

4. Turn right-side out. Fold top raw edge to inside ¼ inch and press. Turn down another ¼ inch and stitch around.

5. Add ribbon all around stocking and across front of top approximately 1 inch down from top. Tie ribbon bow in front if desired. Add ribbon loop to corner of edge opening.

Materials (for stocking ornament)
40 squares of fabric, 1½ x 1½ inches
backing fabric, 6 x 8 inches
eyelet and ribbons if desired (22 inches of each)

Directions
You can make this little stocking ornament from a few leftovers to match the larger stocking or it can be completely different.

Make this as you did the larger stocking. Stitch vertical rows of fabric together in the following way: 1 row of 7 squares, 3 rows of 8, 1 row of 5, 4 rows of 4.

Cut out front and back using the stocking pattern provided same size here. No enlarging is necessary. Finish as with other project. Add ribbon and lace as before.

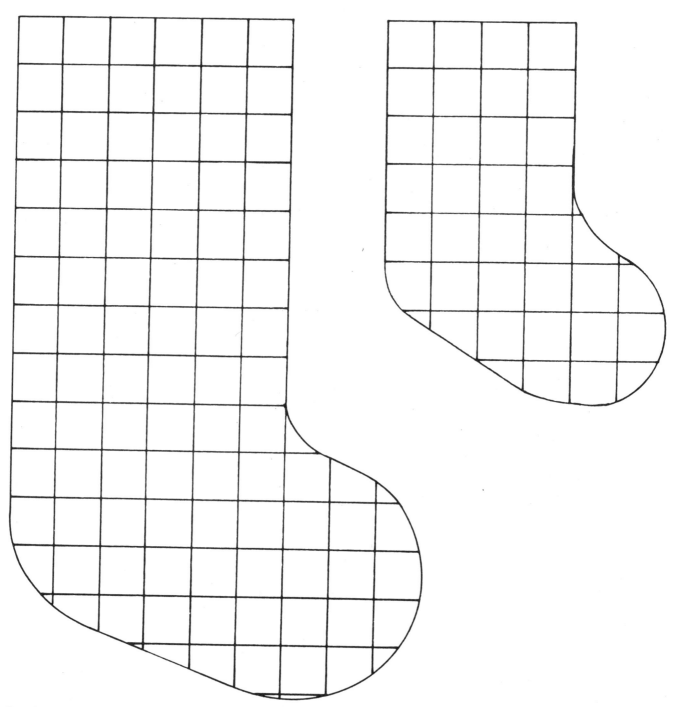

Patchwork stocking and ornament pattern. Each square equals 1 inch.

Elf Stocking

This project reminds me of a jester's stocking and I was tempted to design it with a pointed toe. Christmas protocol dictated a more conventional approach, and my daughter Lisa thinks it looks like an elf's stocking.

At Christmastime most five-and-ten-cent stores carry red and green felt pieces 12 x 18 inches in addition to the usual 9 x 12-inch pieces that come in all colors. This stocking can be made from 2 green and 1 red felt piece. It is not padded. If you'd like to do this, however, add quilt batting to the list of materials and cut 2 pieces of fabric for lining.

Materials

1 piece 12 x 18-inch red felt
2 pieces 12 x 18-inch green felt
6 large bells
white embroidery floss
6 inches ½-inch red ribbon
graph paper
white chalk

Directions

The stocking is 15 inches long. Each square on the grid equals 1 inch. Transfer the pattern to graph paper (page 16). Tape the tracing to a window pane with the green felt piece over this. You should be able to see the outline in order to retrace with the chalk onto the felt.

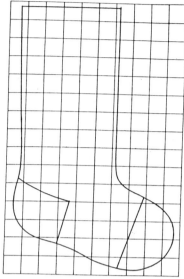

Each square equals 1 inch.

1. Trace the cuff pattern and the heel and toe patterns, which are shown same size. When cutting out all pieces, add a ¼-inch seam allowance. Cut 2 green stocking bodies. From the red felt, cut 2 pieces for the cuff, 2 heels, and 2 toes.
2. Pin the heel and toe in position on the front and back pieces of the stocking as indicated on the pattern. Stitch along the straight edge only of the heel and toe pieces.
3. With wrong sides facing pin the front and back of the stocking together and stitch along the edges leaving top edge open. Trim seams as close to the stitching as possible.
4. Write the person's name on the front of one cuff piece. Use 2 strands of white cotton floss and embroider the name with a running or back stitch (page 15).

To finish

1. Place right sides of the cuff pieces together and stitch side seams.
2. Turn right-side out and place the cuff over the top of the stocking matching top edges. Stitch around ¼ inch from the top.
3. Fold ribbon in half and tack inside top edge of stocking. Attach a large bell to the end of each point of the cuff.

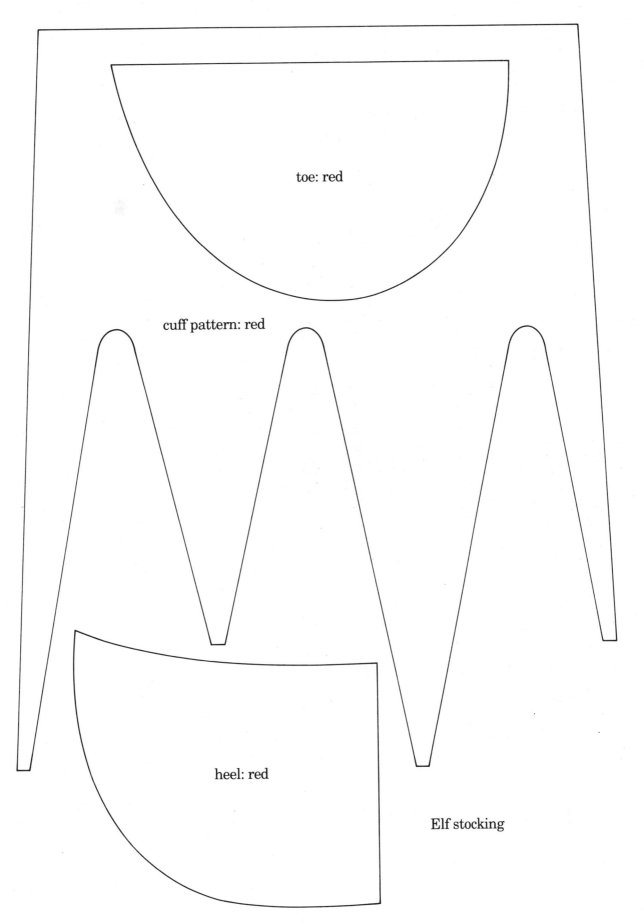

toe: red

cuff pattern: red

heel: red

Elf stocking

Sleepy-Time Doll Stocking

This quilted patchwork stocking is made with scraps of delicate country prints. The front of the stocking looks like the doll's bed. What small child wouldn't be thrilled to find that this tiny doll actually comes out to play? The night before Christmas your child can tuck her doll into bed to wait for Santa's arrival.

Materials (for stocking)
1 white and 1 pink felt square
31 printed fabric squares 1½ inches
small piece black and red embroidery floss
polyester batting
7 x 9½-inch piece of white cotton
5 inches white eyelet
5 inches ⅛-inch pink satin ribbon
pink cotton double-fold bias tape

(for doll)
scraps of light pink, dark pink, cream, and black felt
brown yarn
⅛-inch pink satin ribbon
batting
glue

Directions

All seams are ¼ inch, which you will add when cutting out the pattern. Use this pattern to cut 2 pieces from pink felt. Cut 1 piece of white felt 4 x 5½ inches. Cut 1 piece of batting 6½ x 6½ inches.

1. Arrange and stitch the patchwork squares in vertical rows as follows: 1 row of 3 squares, 2 rows of 4 squares, 4 rows of 5 squares.

2. Place the piece of batting over the 7 x 9½-inch piece of cotton with the extra 3½ inches of cotton at the top. Pin at the edges.

3. Place the row of 5 squares face up on the batting 1½ inches in from the heel edge. Place another row of 5 squares face down on the first strip, matching squares.

4. Stitch inside edge through all layers. Open flat and follow procedure with the remaining strips. Cover the heel side with the strip of 4 squares and the strip of 3 squares. Use the felt pattern to trim all edges.

5. Turn the edge of the cotton down ¼ inch and fold down to cover the raw edge of the quilt. Press. Position the eyelet under the edge of the sheet with a border of ⅛-inch pink ribbon on top of the edge. Stitch across through all layers of material.

To appliqué

Transfer the cat design to white felt and cut out. Pin to the front of the patchwork area where indicated on the drawing. Stitch around outlines with black thread.

To finish

1. Cut a piece of batting 3 x 4½ inches and place this on the top portion of 1 pink felt stocking piece. Pin 4 x 5½-inch piece of white felt on top so top edges of felt match. Stitch across the bottom edge of the white square.

2. Place quilted piece on top of pink and white felt piece with heel and toe matching. Pin this face down to the remaining pink felt backing and stitch around outer edge. Leave top open.

3. Trim seams, clip at curves, and turn to right sides. Turn top edge in ¼ inch and stitch.

4. Bind raw edges with bias tape. Make a hanger for the stocking from 6 inches of bias tape folded in half and stitched. Attach inside stocking.

To make doll

1. Trace doll pattern on cream-colored felt.
2. Place batting between this and another piece of cream felt, and stitch around the outline. Cut out.
3. Trace dress pattern on light pink felt. Cut 2. Cut 2 dark pink pieces for the collar. Stitch front and back of dress together and glue neck pieces to top of dress at front and back. Add a small pocket and eyelet trim to bottom edge. Put dress on doll.
4. Cut 6 strands of brown yarn 10 inches long. Find the center of the yarn and tack to the top of the doll's head. Tack at each side and braid the strands on either side. Tie ends with yarn or satin ribbons. Cut and glue small black felt shoes on feet.
5. Use 3 strands of black embroidery floss to fill in the eyes and 3 strands of red for the mouth. Insert doll into pocket on front of stocking.

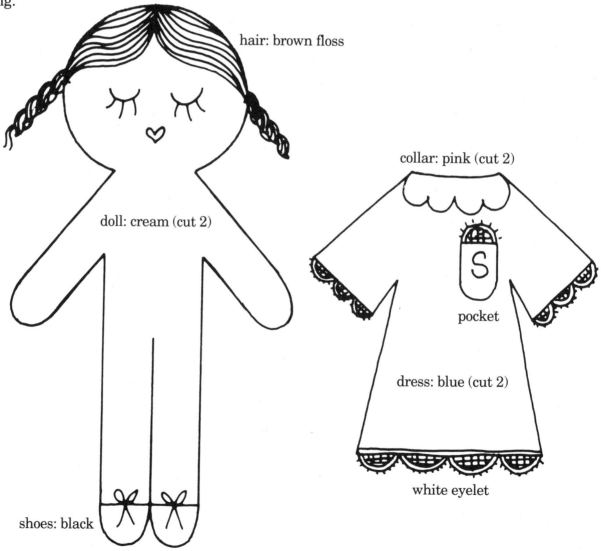

hair: brown floss

doll: cream (cut 2)

shoes: black

collar: pink (cut 2)

pocket

dress: blue (cut 2)

white eyelet

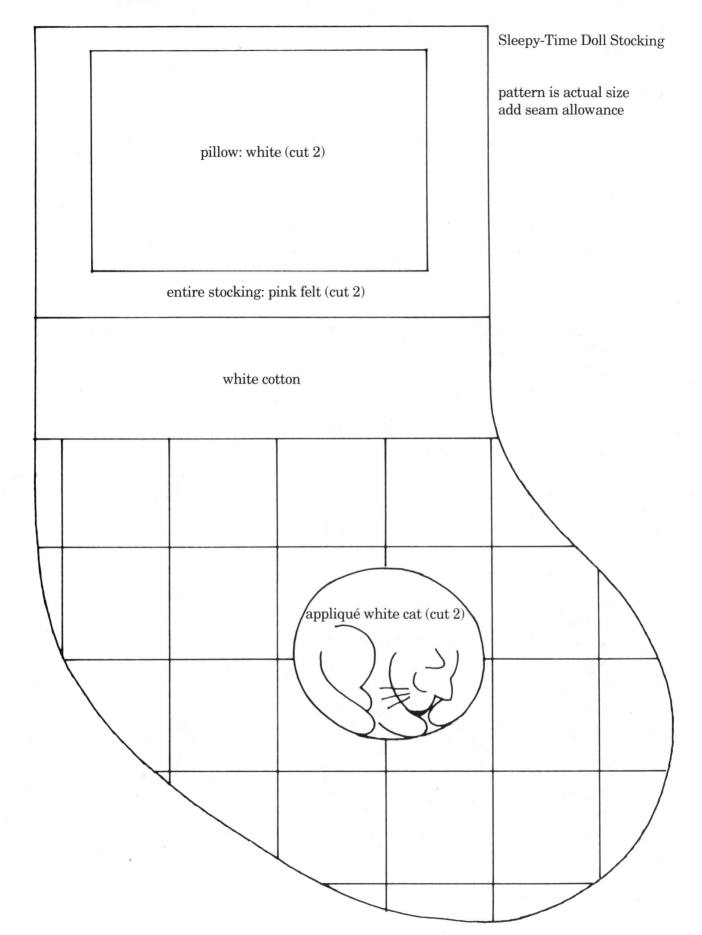

Sleepy-Time Doll Stocking

pattern is actual size
add seam allowance

pillow: white (cut 2)

entire stocking: pink felt (cut 2)

white cotton

appliqué white cat (cut 2)

Babes-in-Toyland Stocking and Ornaments

This needlepoint stocking was designed for a boy or girl, as well as an adult who is young at heart. The Continental stitch is used throughout to create the Alpine design.

A needlepoint stocking is very special. The time and effort put into such projects are well worth the results, which will last forever. Such projects are used year after year and often pass from one generation to another, always a reminder of the loving care that someone put into them.

The pattern for the finished stocking will be 11 inches long.

Materials
11 x 14-inch 10-count canvas
Bernat 1-2-3-ply Persian-type yarn 12½ pull skeins (2 skeins bright blue, 2 bright green, 1½ red, 1 white, and ½ bright yellow)
needle
masking tape
2 pieces 9 x 12-inch royal blue felt

Directions
Tape the edges of the canvas to avoid raveling. Enlarge the design and trace it onto the canvas. Follow the charted diagram for placement of stitches.
1. Work across each row until the front of the stocking is filled in. If the canvas needs blocking, steam it and pull into position. Pin to a wooden board to dry.
2. Cut out the stocking with ¼ inch all around. Use the stocking and trace outline on 1 piece of felt. Cut out 2 blue felt stocking pieces. Pin the 2 felt pieces together, matching edges. Machine-stitch around edge, leaving top open. Clip into curves and turn.
3. Turn the edge of the needlepoint canvas under ¼ inch all around and pin to one layer of felt. Stitch together at edges. Attach a ribbon loop to top corner and hang.

Babes-in-Toyland Ornaments
The soldier and pony ornaments use the same designs as the Babes-in-Toyland Stocking. They are worked on 7-count plastic canvas in the same colors as the designs on the stocking. Bind the edges with a contrasting yarn. The pony has a white binding and the soldier's binding is green. Using designs for various decorations is an easy way to coordinate your Christmas look.

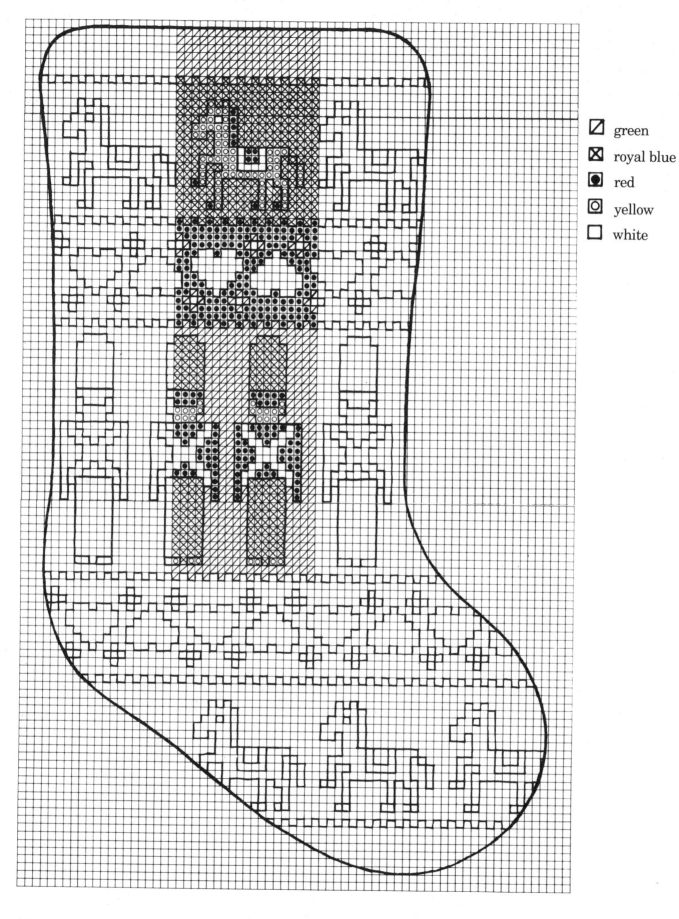

▨	green
⊠	royal blue
◉	red
◎	yellow
☐	white

Santa Stocking & Ornaments

Red and white patchwork has always been a favorite color combination for any quilted project, but it's especially bright and cheerful for a Christmas stocking. Use this easy patchwork theme for a variety of coordinated objects, like a tree skirt, ornaments, and a tablecloth. The right-triangle method is used to make the squares, and then they are arranged in a pinwheel pattern. The stocking is a generous 19 inches long.

Figure 1. Santa Stocking. Each square equals 4 inches.

Materials (45-inch-wide fabric)
½ yard red fabric
½ yard white fabric
½ yard thin quilt batting
tracing paper

Directions
All measurements for cutting include ¼-inch seam allowance.
1. Cut 1 piece of white fabric 14 x 22 inches.
2. Cut 1 piece of red fabric 14 x 22 inches.

Quick-and-Easy Triangle Method
1. On the wrong side of the white rectangle, measure and mark 12 squares 4 x 4 inches.
2. Draw lines diagonally through all squares in the same direction (see below).
3. With right sides facing and raw edges aligned, pin to same-sized piece of red fabric.
4. Stitch ¼ inch on each side of all diagonal lines.
5. Cut on all solid lines. Open seams and press. You will have 24 squares of white and red triangles.

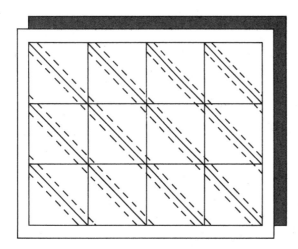

To make rows
1. Refer to Figure 1 for placement of squares. The shaded triangles are red. With right sides facing and raw edges aligned, stitch 2 squares together along one side edge. Open seams and press.
2. Continue to join another square, alternating colors so that you

always stitch a white side to a red side. You now have a row of 3 squares. Make 3 more rows of 3 squares each.

3. Next, join 4 squares to make a row. Make 2 more.

Joining rows

1. Arrange rows as shown in Figure 1. You will have 4 rows of 3 squares followed by 3 rows of 4 squares.

2. With right sides facing and raw edges aligned, join row 1 to row 2 along one long edge, making sure all seams match. Open seams and press. Continue to join rows in this way.

To make stocking

1. Enlarge and transfer the stocking pattern to tracing paper (see Figure 1).

2. Use the pattern piece to cut one from the remaining white fabric, one from remaining red fabric, and one from the quilt batting.

3. Position the stocking pattern on the red and white patchwork piece and cut one.

Quilting

1. Begin by trimming ¼ inch around the quilt batting stocking.

2. Pin or baste the patchwork top, batting, and white lining piece together.

3. Using a small running stitch, quilt ¼ inch on each side of all seam lines. Do not run stitches into outer ¼-inch seam allowance all around.

To finish

1. When all quilting is complete, remove pins or basting stitches.

2. With right sides facing and raw edges aligned, stitch red backing piece to quilted top, leaving top edge open. Clip around curves in seam allowance. Turn right-side out and press.

3. Cut a strip of white fabric 2½ x 16½ inches. (This strip can be made by stitching 2 pieces together if necessary.)

4. Using leftover patchwork scraps, make a hanging loop 1½ x 2½ inches.

5. Hem one long edge of the white strip of fabric.

6. Join the short ends of the white strip to make a loop.

7. With right sides facing and raw edges aligned, pin the white strip to the top edge of the stocking. Slip the raw ends of the loop between the fabric at the long seam of the stocking.

8. Stitch around. Turn white lining strip to the inside of the

stocking and pull loop up. Press and stay-stitch around top as close to the edge as possible.

Red and White Ornaments

Create a bunch of ornaments to match the stocking. It's easy to make several at once. Each ornament is made from one red and white square.

Directions

1. Use the Quick-and-Easy Triangle Method (page 22) to mark and cut as many squares as needed.
2. Back each square with a piece of thin quilt batting and take small running stitches ¼ inch on each side of the center seam line.
3. With right sides facing and raw edges aligned, stitch the front and back squares together around 3 sides and 4 corners.
4. Turn right-side out, stuff, and stitch opening closed. Add a hanging loop.

Christmas Ornaments

Cookie Cutter Ornaments

These cookie cutter ornaments can be made with leftover scraps of colorful fabric. Scraps of patchwork fabric for some of the ornaments add real country charm to your tree.

Materials
scraps of calico
fusible webbing
tracing paper
stiff paper
green, red, or gold cord for hanging

Directions
1. Trace and transfer all shapes to stiff paper.
2. Trace all pattern pieces for the individual ornaments from these pages.
3. Pin each pattern piece to a scrap of fabric on top of a piece of fusible webbing. Cut out each piece.
4. Position each pattern piece of fabric and fusible webbing on the cardboard ornament and fuse with a medium-hot iron.

To finish
1. To add details such as the buttons on the gingerbread man, cut small circles of felt or use tiny buttons and glue in position.
2. You can glue rickrack around the hearts if desired, or add lace, ribbon, eyelet, etc.
3. Poke a hole near the top of each ornament and thread cord through each. Tie to make a hanging loop.
4. The back of each ornament can be finished as you did the front, or you can simply cut a solid piece of fabric, using the shape as a pattern. Fuse to the back as you did the front pieces.

Cookie Cutter Ornament patterns

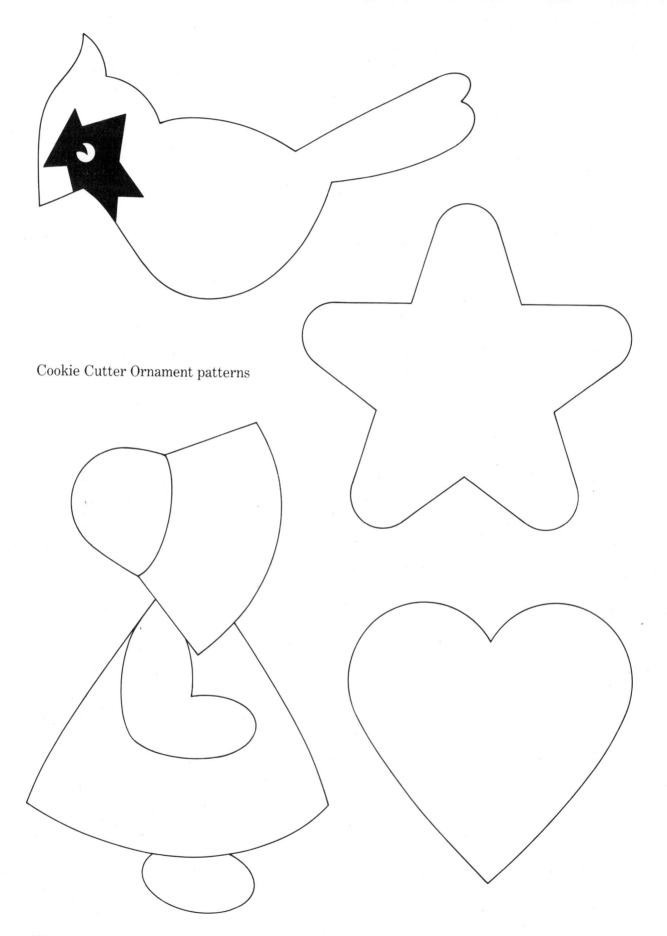

Cookie Cutter Ornament patterns

Three Bears,
Angel Cat, Cool Cats

Children will love helping you make these lovable characters.

Papa Bear

Materials
2 pieces 9 x 12-inch caramel-colored felt squares for 4 bears
scrap of red and black felt
black thread
paper punch
polyester batting
small piece of black embroidery floss

Directions
Trace the bear pattern 4 times on 1 piece of caramel felt. Trace the coat pattern 4 times on red and the pants 4 times on black.
1. Sandwich batting between the two pieces of caramel felt with the outline of each bear on top. Stitch around each outline with black thread. Cut out each body as close to stitches as possible.
2. Cut out 2 layers of felt for each pair of pants and stitch the 2 pieces together at side edges. Turn right side out and slip onto the bottom of each bear.
3. Cut out each red coat and put on each bear. Use the paper punch to make a black button and glue each in position on the coats.
4. Embroider each face with 2 strands of black floss and add a hanging loop at the top of each head.

Mama Bear

Materials
2 pieces 9 x 12-inch caramel-colored felt squares for 4 bears
2 pieces blue felt
scraps of white, pink, and red felt
scrap of lace
black embroidery floss
black thread
glue
polyester batting

Directions
Trace the bear pattern 4 times on 1 piece of caramel felt. Trace the body of the dress 4 times on blue felt. Trace apron pattern 4 times on white, and cut out small pieces for pockets, collars, buttons, and bottom trim of dress.

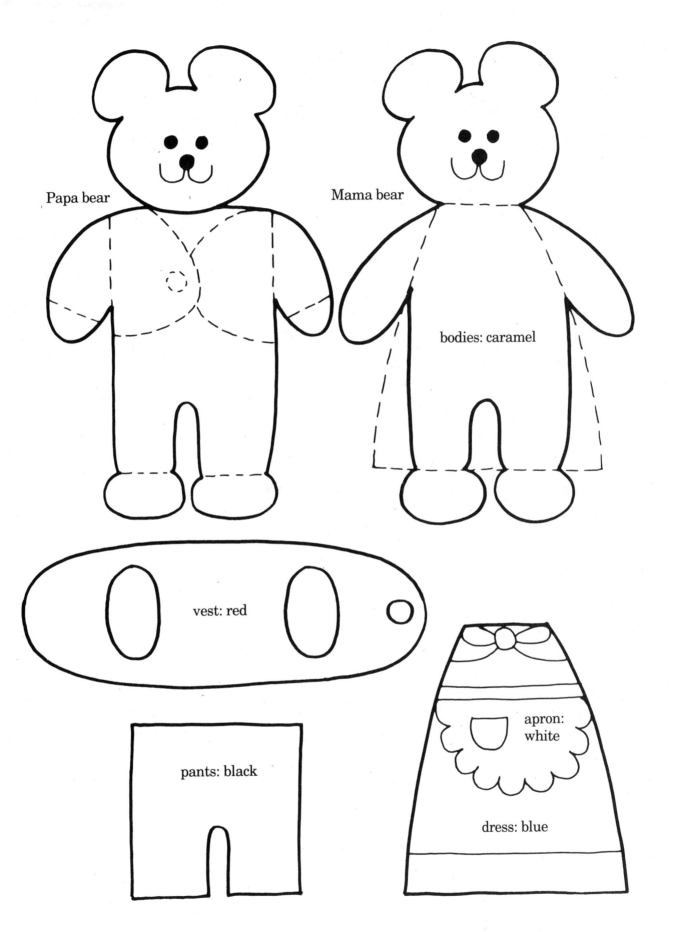

Papa bear

Mama bear

bodies: caramel

vest: red

apron: white

pants: black

dress: blue

137

1. Place felt with outlines of each bear on top of 1 layer of batting and another piece of caramel felt. Stitch around the outline and cut each out close to stitches.

2. Place blue felt pattern on another layer of felt and cut out 2 for each bear. No batting between layers.

3. With 1 dress piece on the front and back of each bear, stitch around edges. Glue apron and details to front of dress. Add lace trim over arms on either side of dress.

4. Use 2 strands of black floss to embroider details on each face. Add hanging loop.

body: mustard (cut 2)

Baby Bear

Materials

2 pieces 9 x 12-inch mustard-color felt squares
scraps of pink, black, and red felt
glue
black thread
small piece red and black embroidery thread
paper punch
4 lollipops

Directions

Trace 4 bear patterns (page 138) on one piece of felt. Pin this to a second piece of felt with batting between. Stitch around the outline of each pattern and where arms, legs, and head join body. Stitch face or hand-embroider.

Cut out each ornament. Use the paper punch to make red felt buttons and pink inside-ear parts. Cut a black piece for the nose. Clip edge of pink circles to fit. (See finished drawing.) Glue buttons, ears, and nose in position. Tie a piece of red embroidery thread around the neck and tack a loop to the top for hanging.

Fold end of one arm around a lollipop stick and tack it to itself. Hang several of these teddy bears on your tree for the children who come to visit.

Angel Cat

While not your traditional pussy cat, this angel is every bit as adorable. You might even want to make several!

Materials

caramel, white, pale pink, and bright pink felt pieces
polyester batting
black and white thread
6 inches of pink embroidery floss
small piece of black floss
3 inches of eyelet

Directions

Trace the pattern for each piece onto felt. The colors for each piece are indicated on the pattern.
1. With batting sandwiched between 2 pieces of felt, stitch around head and arm pieces. Cut out as close to stitches as possible. Black stitches accentuate the outline of these parts.

2. With batting between 2 pieces of white felt, stitch along side edges below wings and across the bottom. Cut this out. Sandwich batting between wing pieces and stitch around outline. Cut out.

3. Insert arm and wing pieces on either side of body and insert neck of head into the top. Stitch all open edges.

4. Cut one piece of bright pink scalloped edge and place a piece of eyelet even with the top edge. Stitch this to the underside of the bottom edge of body.

To finish

Embroider the face with 3 strands of black embroidery floss in a backstitch and use French knots for eyes. Tie a pink embroidery thread bow around the neck and attach a hanging loop at top corner of body.

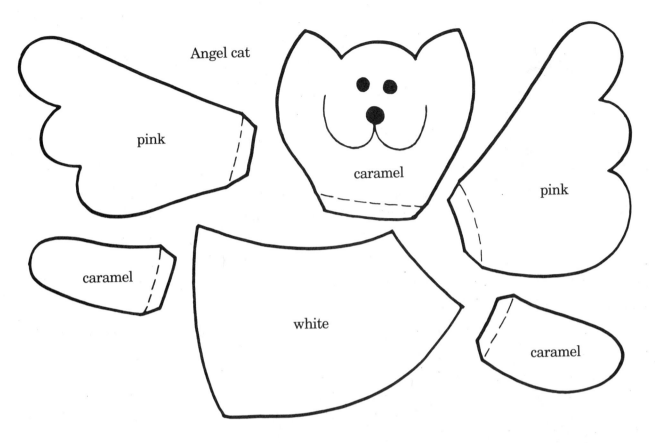

Angel cat

pink

caramel

pink

caramel

white

caramel

Cool Cats
Add these characters to your tree for a bit of whimsy.

Materials
2 9 x 12-inch light brown felt squares for 4 ornaments
2 9 x 12-inch red felt squares
scrap of white felt
black and red thread
black embroidery floss
polyester batting
glue

Directions
Trace 4 cat patterns on brown felt and 4 coats on red felt.
1. Sandwich batting between the 2 brown pieces and stitch around each cat with black thread. Cut out close to stitches.
2. Cut a double thickness for each coat (not batting). Place the one-piece coat on front, with another piece on the back of each cat, and stitch around edges with red thread.
3. Fill in eye and nose area with black thread and stitch with 1 strand in a backstitch along the mouth lines.

Cat in the hat

Cut and stitch cat pattern as above. Cut double layer of red coats and hats. Cut strips of white felt for coats and hats.

1. Place coat and hat pieces on the front and back of each cat and stitch around the outer edges with red thread. The hat can be glued to the head.

2. Glue strips onto front and back of red felt.

3. Add a hanging loop to the top of each and stitch face details as above.

Cool cats

bodies: light brown

coat: red

stitches

stitches

coat and hat: red and white

Magical Mystical Stars and Moon

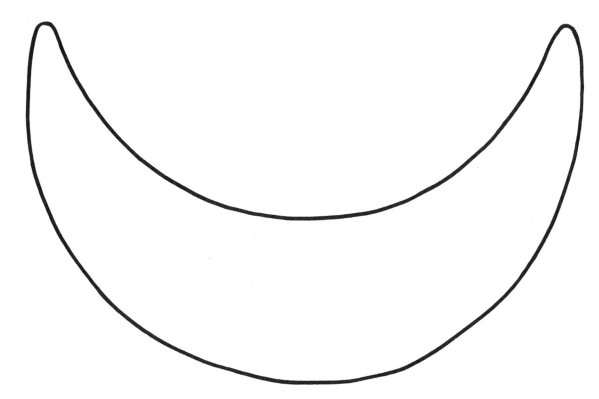

Pattern for Magical Mystical Moon

Cover your tree with stars and moons encircled in clouds. It's so
easy to make these brightly colored felt stars in different sizes.
The largest will encircle the bottom of the tree and gradually get
smaller toward the top.

Materials
a number of felt squares in a variety of colors
polyester fiberfill fat batting
thread to match felt

Directions
The patterns are given full-size. Trace each size on plain paper
and cut out to use as a template. Outline the star on felt colors
as many times as desired. Do not cut out.
1. Sandwich a piece of batting between 1 layer of felt and the felt
with a star outline on top. Pin together. Machine-stitch through
all 3 layers just inside the pencil line.
2. Cut out each felt layer of the star separately at the pencil line.
Do not cut through the batting.
3. Gently pull away the batting so there is an outline of fluff
around every point on the star.
4. Attach a loop of embroidery floss to match each star and hang.

144

Pattern for Magical Mystical Stars and Ribbon Stars

Ribbon Stars

Make a batch of ribbon stars from your scraps of ribbon! They can be as gay as you want, combining a variety of colors, designs, and patterns. Or choose a color combination of red and green or pastels and make all the stars match. Ribbon comes in strips and dots as well, for another variation. Use whatever ribbons you use on the ornaments for all your packages too. This will give you an interesting theme and will solve all your decorating problems.

Materials
small piece of muslin
small piece of felt
several strips of multicolored ½-inch ribbon
scissors
pins
Poly-Fil
needle and thread

Directions
Trace the star pattern (page 16) and transfer it to the muslin. Place this over the felt and cut out 2 stars.
1. Pin strips of ribbon across the front of the muslin star. Stitch along each edge. If you prefer, you can cut a piece of fusible

webbing from the star pattern. Place this between the muslin and ribbons and iron in place. No stitching necessary.

2. Place the felt star on top of the ribbon star and stitch around the edges, leaving an opening for turning. Clip around each star point.

3. Turn the star right-side out and press. Stuff with Poly-Fil until the star is very full. Use a pointed object to push the stuffing into each point. A blunt pencil or crochet hook is good for this purpose.

4. Slip-stitch the opening and add a piece of string, yarn, or ribbon for hanging.

Making in quantity

You can easily make a wide variety of these ornaments by first creating your ribbon fabric from all the odds and ends of ribbon you can find. Simply sew strips of ribbon to the muslin until you have enough material from which you can cut the number of stars desired.

Make a template of cardboard for the star pattern. Place this on the back of the ribbon-covered muslin and draw around it with a soft pencil as many times as needed. Pin this to a piece of felt the same size, and cut out all stars before sewing together as above.

Heart-Warming Hearts

Puffy patchwork hearts make the perfect sachets, Christmas ornaments, or decorations for almost anywhere. The Amish use old pieces of quilts to make projects like this. However, if you don't have an old quilt to serve the purpose, it's easy to piece fabric together for small projects. If you use 100 percent cotton and wash the fabric first, when quilted, it will have the character found in old quilts. For a faded look, add a little bleach to the wash.

Materials
piece of blue fabric 8 x 12 inches
piece of white fabric 8 x 12 inches
pieces of muslin 12 x 12 inches
stuffing
1 yard ¼-inch blue satin ribbon
thin quilt batting
tracing paper

Directions

All measurements include ¼-seam allowance. The following directions are for the quick-and-easy right-triangle method of joining triangles of 2 different colors (see diagram on page 22).

1. Measure and mark 12 squares, each 2½ x 2½ inches on the wrong side of the white fabric (3 rows of 4 squares each).

2. Draw a diagonal line through all squares.

3. With right sides facing and raw edges aligned, pin the white fabric to the same size piece of blue fabric.

4. Stitch ¼ inch on each side of the diagonal lines, through both thicknesses.

5. Cut on all solid lines. Open seams and press. You will have 24 squares made from blue and white triangles.

To make patchwork

You can arrange the squares so the triangles all go in the same direction or in different directions, whatever looks best to you.

1. With right sides facing and raw edges aligned, stitch 2 squares together along one side edge. Next, join another square.

2. Make 8 rows of 3 squares each.

3. With right sides facing, stitch 2 rows together along the bottom edge. Open seams and press. Continue to join rows in this way.

To make hearts

1. Trace the heart pattern in Figure 1 and cut out 1 large and 2 small hearts.

2. Pin the pattern pieces to the muslin and cut 2 for each heart.

3. Pin the pattern pieces to the patchwork fabric and cut 1 for each heart.

4. Pin the pattern pieces to the batting and cut 1 for each heart.

To quilt

1. Pin a patchwork heart to the batting and then to a muslin heart.

2. Using small running stitches, quilt ⅛ inch on each side of all seam lines, stopping before seam allowance all around. Remove pins.

To finish

1. With right sides facing and raw edges aligned, pin the quilted top to the remaining muslin backing piece and stitch around, leaving 2 inches open on one side edge.

2. Clip around seam allowance.
3. Turn right-side out and stuff firmly.
4. Turn raw edges to inside and slip-stitch opening closed.
5. Arrange the hearts with the large heart between the 2 smaller ones; hand-stitch the ribbon across the back of all 3.
6. Tie a bow at each end and hang.

Figure 1

Calico Tree Treasures

These star ornaments are made by folding contrasting fabrics to create points. They are easier to make than they look. Rectangles are folded into triangles and then attached to a backing fabric with the patches radiating out to cover a small area. This is why the design is so interesting for Christmas ornaments. If you don't add a hanging loop, they could be used as pin cushions.

Materials (for a green, red, and blue ornament)
small amounts of red, blue, and green calico
small amounts of solid red, blue, and green fabric
small amount of muslin
5 x 5-inch piece of each solid color for backing of each ornament
package of red, blue, and green piping for each ornament
6 inches of ¼-inch-wide ribbon for each ornament
stuffing

Directions
All measurements include ¼-inch seam allowance.

Cut the following:
12 strips, each 1½ x 2½ inches from each calico print
8 strips, each 1½ x 2½ inches from each solid fabric

24 strips, each 1½ x 2½ inches from muslin

To prepare patches

1. With the wrong side up, turn the long edge of each strip up ¼ inch and press.

2. Find the center of the opposite edge and bring the 2 corners at each end of the folded edge down to meet at this point. You will have created a triangular shape. Press. This is the front of the patch (see Figure 1). Prepare all strips of fabric in this way.

3. Using a light pencil, draw a diagonal line across the muslin backing. Draw a diagonal line in the opposite direction. Draw a line across the center of the square in each direction. The backing is now divided into 8 equal parts.

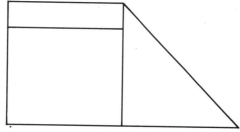

Figure 1. Fold corners of rectangle to middle to create triangle-shaped piece.

Round 1

The directions that follow are for the red and blue ornaments, which start with calico patches. For the green ornament, start with solid patches in the center, followed by calico, then solid, etc.

1. Use 4 patches of the same calico color for the first round and pin one to the backing fabric as shown in Figure 2.

2. Tack the point to the backing, then take small slip-stitches on either side of the point to hold the patch in place. Attach the other 3 patches in the same way, making sure they meet in the center.

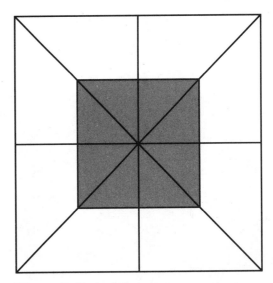

Figure 2. Round 1

Round 2

1. Use 8 muslin patches for the second round. Pin and tack 4 patches in the same way as in Round 1, so the points are approximately ¾ inch from the center where the calico points come together.

2. The remaining 4 patches overlap the first 4 of this round. Tack in position as in Round 1 (see Figure 3).

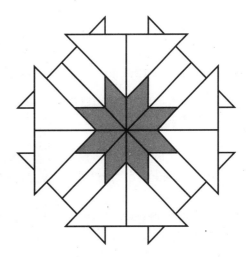

Figure 3. Round 2

Round 3

1. Using 8 calico patches, place them between the patches of the previous round so the points touch the outer points of the star

shape made by the previous round (Figure 4).
2. Pin and stitch these patches in place as in Round 1.

Figure 4. Round 3

Round 4

1. Using 8 solid patches, pin in the same way as in Round 2, pinning the first 4 patches to align with the 4 patches from Round 2.
2. Pin the next 4 patches to align with the other 4 patches from Round 2.

To finish

1. With right sides facing and raw edges aligned, pin the piping around the outside edge of the pieced fabric.
2. Stitch around.
3. Fold the ribbon in half lengthwise to make a 3-inch loop and pin raw ends to the raw edge of the fabric with the loop on the fabric.
4. Cut backing same size as pieced top. With right sides facing and raw edges aligned, pin top and backing together with ribbon between.
5. Stitch around the edges, leaving a small opening for turning.
6. Trim seam allowance, turn right-side out, and stuff firmly. Slip-stitch opening closed.

Mini-Stocking Ornaments

I always like to present projects to make from scraps of fabric, but the scraps never really get all used up, so I like to have projects from the scraps of the scraps. These mini-stockings (Figure 1) will use up your tiniest pieces of fabric and make good bazaar sellers as well as gifts. Tuck coins or a tiny prize inside for young children.

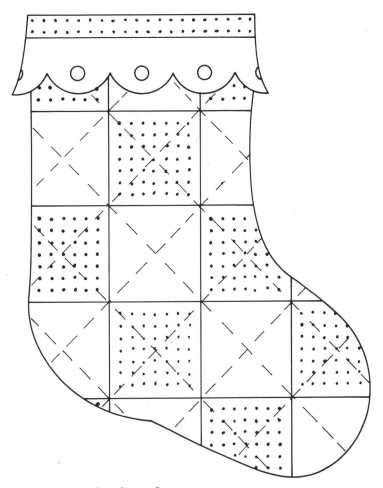

Figure 1. Mini-Stocking Ornaments

Materials
small pieces of red prints
small pieces of bleached muslin (or white fabric)
thin quilt batting
12 inches ¼-inch red ribbon
6 inches 1-inch-wide pregathered white eyelet
tracing paper

Directions

All measurements include ¼-inch seam allowance.

Cut the following:

12 red squares 1½ x 1½ inches each
12 muslin squares 1½ x 1½ inches each

1. Trace and cut out the stocking pattern.
2. Use this pattern to cut 3 pieces from muslin and 2 from the quilt batting.

To make patchwork

1. With right sides facing and raw edges aligned, join a muslin square to a red square along one edge. Open seams and press.
2. Continue to join alternating squares to make a row of 8.
3. Start the second row with a red square, then a muslin square, and continue to join alternating squares to make a row of 8. Make 6 rows in this way.
4. With right sides facing and raw edges aligned, join all 6 rows to make a piece of patchwork fabric 4½ x 6½ inches.
5. Pin the stocking pattern (Figure 2) to the patchwork fabric. Cut one.

To quilt

1. Pin the patchwork top to one piece of batting and then to a corresponding piece of muslin.
2. Using small running stitches, quilt across the fabric on the diagonal, from one corner of each square to the other, across the entire piece of fabric.
3. Pin the 2 back muslin pieces together with the batting between.
4. Draw a 1-inch grid on the diagonal across the back fabric and quilt as for the front.

To finish

1. With right sides facing and raw edges aligned, stitch around, leaving the top edge open.
2. Trim seams as close to stitch line as possible and turn right-side out.
3. Turn top, raw edges to the inside, and stitch around top edge.
4. Stitch the white eyelet around the top edge of the stocking.
5. Next, stitch red ribbon over the top edge of the eyelet.
6. Cut a 5-inch length of ribbon and fold it in half to form a loop. Attach inside the top of the stocking for hanging.

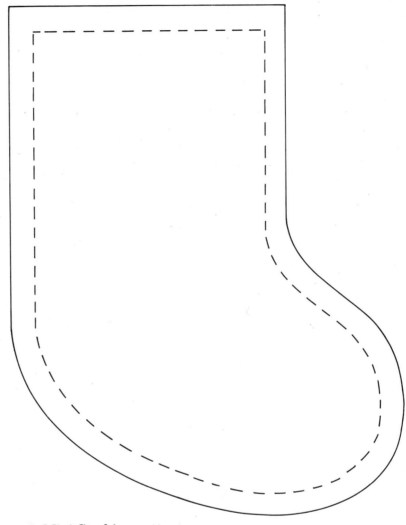

Figure 2. Mini-Stocking pattern

Stitch-'n'-Stuff Stars

Since so many ornaments are needed to decorate the Christmas tree, it's always fun and practical to make many at once. If you can use up your scrap fabrics, it is also inexpensive. I like to use one shape, such as a star, and vary it with the combination of fabric colors and prints (see photograph in color section). In this way you have a variety of designs, but the technique is the same for all.

Patchwork star ornaments make wonderful items for selling at a Christmas bazaar. If you're going to parties over the holidays, take along a handmade ornament.

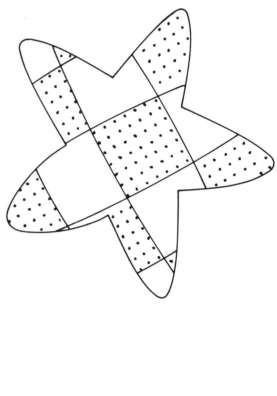

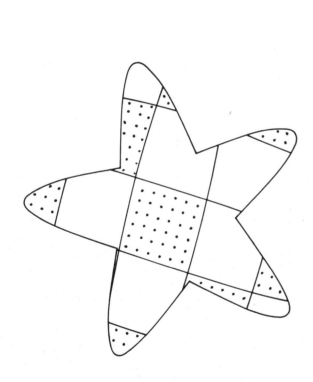

Materials
scraps of red, blue, and calico fabric
backing fabric 8 x 8 inches for each star ornament
stuffing
tracing paper
ribbon or embroidery floss for hanging